Energy Efficient Buildings

Architecture, Engineering, and Environment

Dean Hawkes and Wayne Forster

Energy Efficient Buildings

Architecture, Engineering, and Environment

Dean Hawkes and Wayne Forster

W·W·NORTON

NEW YORK · LONDON

For information about permission to reproduce selections from this book,
write to Permissions, W. W. Norton & Company, Inc., 500 Fifth Avenue, New York, NY 10110

The text of this book is composed in Univers
Manufacturing by C&C Offset Printing Co. Ltd.
Book design by Frank Philippin at Brighten the Corners, London

Library of Congress Cataloging-in-Publication Data

Hawkes, Dean.
  Energy efficient building : architecture, engineering, and environment
/ Dean Hawkes and Wayne Forster.
    p. cm.
Includes bibliographical references and index.
  ISBN 0-393-73092-1
  1. Architecture and energy conservation. 2. Buildings--Environmental
engineering. I. Forster, Wayne. II. Title.
  NA2542.3 .H39 2002
  720'.472--dc21
                                                  2002002021

W. W. Norton & Company, Inc., 500 Fifth Avenue, New York, N.Y. 10110
www.wwnorton.com

W.W. Norton & Company Ltd., Castle House, 75/76 Wells Street, London W1T 3QT

0 9 8 7 6 5 4 3 2 1

Frontispiece: Marzahn Low-energy Apartment Building,
Berlin; architects: Assmann, Salomon & Scheidt;
photographer: Christian Gahl

Contents

Introduction

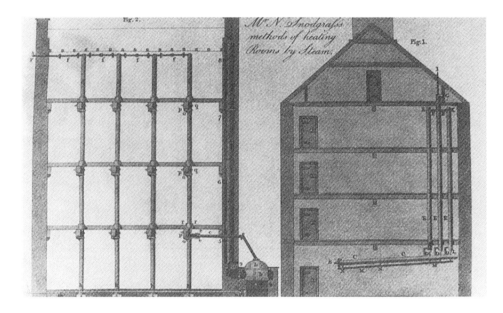

'The Engineer, inspired by the law of Economy and governed by mathematical calculation, puts us in accord with universal law. He achieves harmony. The Architect, by his arrangement of forms, realises an order which is a pure creation of his spirit; by forms and shapes he affects our senses to an acute degree and provokes plastic emotions; by the relationships which he creates he wakes profound echoes in us, he gives us the measure of an order which we feel to be in accordance with that of our world, he determines the various movements of our hearts and of our understanding; it is then that we experience the sense of beauty.'

In one of the seminal statements of the Modern Movement in architecture, Le Corbusier, writing in 1923, defines the relationship between the realms of the engineer and the architect.[1] The engineer, using 'the law of Economy' and the tools of 'mathematical calculation', is engaged with the 'universal' and, in this, appeals to the intellect. By contrast, the architect by 'his arrangement of forms' gives us the measure of 'an order' which we feel, and thereby affects our senses and emotions. Together, it is implied, they hold one of the keys to the creation of a new architecture by offering a synthesis of logic and intuition. As Le Corbusier had foreseen, the design of almost all modern buildings involves a partnership between the engineer and the architect, while the craft tradition that served as the technical foundation of architecture for much of its history has been swept away by increasingly complex and sophisticated construction technologies.

↓
fig. 3: Cockle-stove
heating system, late
18th century;. after
Bruegmann.

↓
fig. 4: William Cook,
steam heating
system, 1784; after
Bruegmann.

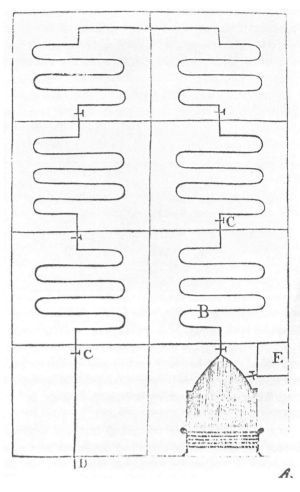

The aim of this book is to examine the nature of the evolving relationship between engineering and architecture in transforming the environmental function and performance of buildings and to illustrate examples of the best contemporary practice. Arup was the engineer for each of these. We begin with an outline of the emergence of architectural engineering as it developed during the early years of the Industrial Revolution and illustrate its influence on both the theory and practice of architecture in the 19th century. This is followed by a review of the way in which the founders of the Modern Movement redefined the functional and formal relationships between the structure, enclosure and systems of buildings in the early decades of the 20th century. From this foundation we trace the way in which the objectives and methods of environmental control have developed further as the complex relationship between art and technology has unfolded.

The second half of the book examines the situation at the beginning of the 21st century, when the debate about the vulnerability of the global environment has given new significance to the environmental agenda in architecture. This review consists of a sequence of critical studies of recent building projects, drawn from around the world, which show how a new-found creative collaboration between architecture and engineering can produce designs that combine logic and intuition in solving increasingly complex and demanding tasks.

fig. 5: Robert Adam, Edinburgh Register Office, showing Perkins hot-water-heating system, installed 1837; after Bruegmann.

Industrialization and the transformation of architecture

Nikolaus Pevsner, in *Pioneers of Modern Design*,[2] and Sigfried Giedion, in *Space, Time and Architecture*,[3] argue that the emergence of the 'new' architecture of the 20th century had its origins in the industrialization of iron production that took place in the 18th century. Giedion wrote, 'The Industrial Revolution, the abrupt increase in production brought about during the eighteenth century by the introduction of the factory system and the machine, changed the whole appearance of the world, far more so than the social revolution in France.'

The two writers explain how production and design methods were developed and refined as the lessons of the first iron-bridge structures were put to use in the design of buildings. They describe the first iron-framed industrial buildings and the gradual application of the new technology to designs with more self-conscious, and perhaps more pretentious, architectural aspirations. For example, Giedion contrasts Matthew Boulton's and James Watt's utilitarian – but, for its date, remarkably refined – design for an iron-framed cotton mill at Salford, 1799–1801 (fig. 1), with John Nash's cast-iron, palm-tree columns in the kitchen of the Royal Pavilion at Brighton in 1818 (fig. 2).

In France the implications of the industrial society were given formal and political acknowledgment by the foundation in 1794, during the Revolution, of L'Ecole Polytechnique. The school's aim was to provide students with a foundation in theoretical and practical science as an

fig. 6: Sir John
Soane, 12–14
Lincoln's Inn Fields,
London, 1792–1825,
ground floor plan;
after Willmert.

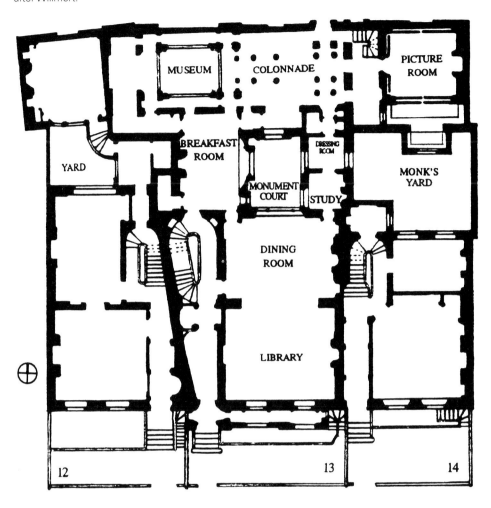

introduction to the specialist courses offered by higher technical schools such as L'Ecole des Ponts et Chaussées and L'Ecole des Mines. But 12 years later, in 1806, Napoleon founded L'Ecole des Beaux-Arts, in effect a revival of an institution of the ancien régime, to cover the entire field of the 'plastic arts', including architecture. This had the effect of formalizing the distinction between architecture as a conservative and primarily artistic pursuit and the new engineering – with practical and intellectual consequences that survived almost to the present day.

By the middle of the 19th century, when the new methods of construction were being confidently exploited in the design of ever more ambitious structures, particularly for new building types such as railway stations and exhibition halls, the distinction between the engineer and the architect had been firmly established.

With hindsight it seems curious that Pevsner and Giedion, the great historians of the origins of the Modern Movement, based their claims for the authority of technology entirely on an account of the use of the new material, structure and construction methods, in other words on the tectonic aspects of architecture. This may perhaps be explained by the way in which these new methods progressively replaced traditional methods in the buildings of the 19th century: sometimes they were visible, as in the great engineering structures; at other times they were discreetly concealed within the shells of more decorous designs. But the development of new structural

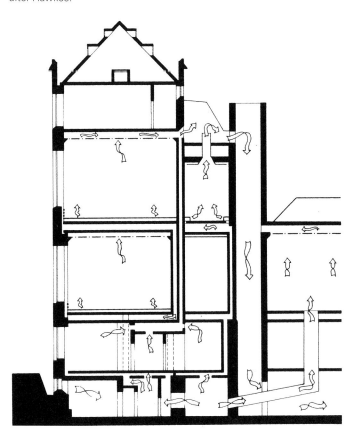

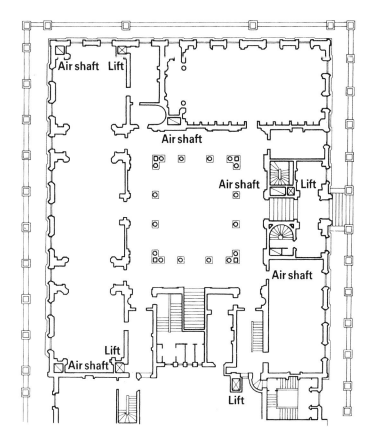

methods and materials was paralleled from the outset by equally significant inventions in the field of what is now called mechanical services.

The first general attempt to bring the technology of environmental control into the historiography of modern architecture came in 1969 with the publication of Banham's *The Architecture of theWell-tempered Environment.*[4] 'In a world more humanely disposed, and more conscious of where the prime human responsibilities of architects lie, the chapters that follow would need no apology, and probably would never need to be written,' he writes. 'It would have been apparent long ago that the art and business of creating buildings is not divisible into two intellectually separate parts – structures, on the one hand, and on the other mechanical services.... Yet architectural history as it has been written up till the present time has seen no reason to apologise or explain away a division that makes no sense in the way buildings are used and paid for by the human race, a division into structure, which is held to be valuable and discussible, and mechanical servicing, which has been almost entirely excluded from historical discussion.' Banham's book provides a indispensable background to a full understanding of the dialogue between architecture and environmental engineering, but in the 30 years since it was written new scholarship has offered further insights into early experiments into methods for the warming, ventilation and artificial lighting of buildings, which began before the end of the 18th century. It has also shown how

↓
fig. 9: H. L. Elmes,
architect, David
Boswell Reid,
engineer, St.
George's Hall,
Liverpool, 1841–54,
cross-section
showing ventilation
ducts; after Olley.

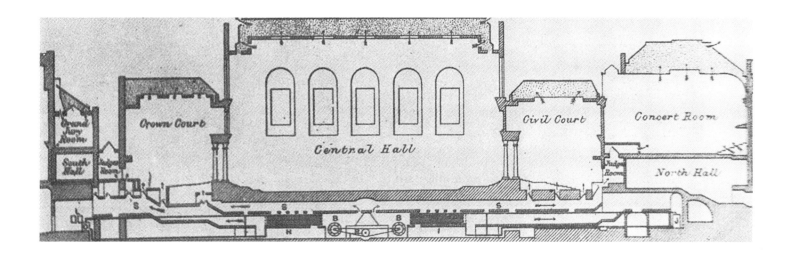

the relationship between architecture and engineering has evolved to create a basis for collaboration in the production of increasingly complex buildings.

Origins: technology and architecture in the 19th century

In one of the standard works on the general history of technology, Derry and Williams propose that the period from 1750 to 1900 was a critical phase in the development of new industrial methods and products and in their practical application.[5] It was during this time that the power of steam was harnessed, coal-gas production was invented and the generation of electricity was perfected. Derry and Williams write that, over these years, 'Western man...was fully entitled to say that his relationship with natural resources had been profoundly changed.' In Britain the education of the engineer was approached much more pragmatically than in France. The existence of engineering as a distinct profession was first acknowledged with the foundation, in 1771, of a society of engineers, which later became the Smeatonian Club, and by the establishment of the Institution of Civil Engineers in 1818. During the 1820s mechanics institutes were established in many of the industrial cities, with the aim of teaching the fundamentals of applied science to workmen. The first chair of engineering in Britain was established in 1840 at the University of Glasgow, followed a year later by a chair at University College, London.

The first 'environmental service', in its modern definition, to be introduced to buildings was control of heating

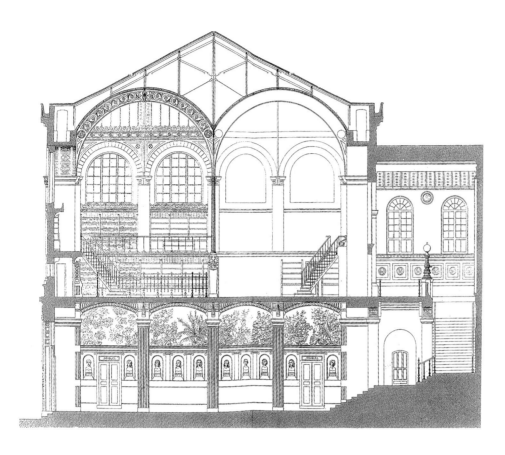

and ventilation. Robert Bruegmann has charted the early development of methods of heating and ventilation towards the end of the 18th century and their rapid development and application in the first half of the 19th century.[6] Most of this took place in Great Britain at a time when increasing industrialization created both needs and opportunities for the application of innovative technologies.

Bruegmann suggests that the earliest modern central-heating installations were based on the distribution of warmed air from solid-fuelled furnaces known as 'cockle stoves' through networks of ducts incorporated in floor and wall construction (fig. 3). These probably had their origins in systems developed for heating horticultural glasshouses, but in 1792 William Strutt used a system of this kind to heat a new mill building at Derby and provided a similar installation in the Derby Infirmary building in 1806. Similar systems continued in use in many types of building for much of the 19th century.

An alternative method, which quickly became popular, was steam heating. The principles of this had been demonstrated as early as 1745 by William Cook, who published a diagram for a system distributing steam from a boiler around a building through a looped configuration of pipes (fig. 4). Again, this was first applied to industrial buildings in the last years of the 18th century. It appears that the mill at Salford by Matthew Boulton and James Watt, which had such significance for Giedion as a precursor of 20th-century

Modernism was, undetected by him, equally significant in the history of environmental design. The hollow cast-iron columns so admired by Giedion formed part of a heat-distribution network.

Later than warm air and steam systems came the adoption of hot water as a heat-distribution medium. The early hot-water systems operated at relatively low temperatures and therefore required large-diameter pipes. In 1831, however, Jacob Perkins, an American engineer working in London, patented a pressurized hot-water system which operated at high temperatures and allowed smaller pipes to be used. This made hot-water heating much more practical and systems quickly became commonplace in buildings of architectural consequence. Among these was Robert Adam's Edinburgh Register Office, built between 1772 and 1792, where a Perkins system was installed in 1837 to replace the original and unsatisfactory warm-air 'hypocaust' (fig. 5).

Sir John Soane, arguably the most important British architect of his day, was keenly interested in the potential of the new methods of heating buildings. He first used a system of steam heating at Tyringham Hall in Buckinghamshire, built between 1793 and 1800. Todd Willmert gives a detailed account of how the question of heating played a crucial role in the development of many of Soane's designs.[7] The most important examples are his works at the Bank of England (from 1792), the Dulwich Picture Gallery (from 1811) and at 12–14 Lincoln's Inn Fields (fig. 6), where the transformation, between

↓
fig. 12: Gottfried
Semper, Hofburg
Theatre, Vienna,
1874, plan.

→
fig. 13: Le Corbusier,
*Cinque points d'une
architecture nouvelle*,
1925; after Le
Corbusier, *Oeuvre
Complet.*

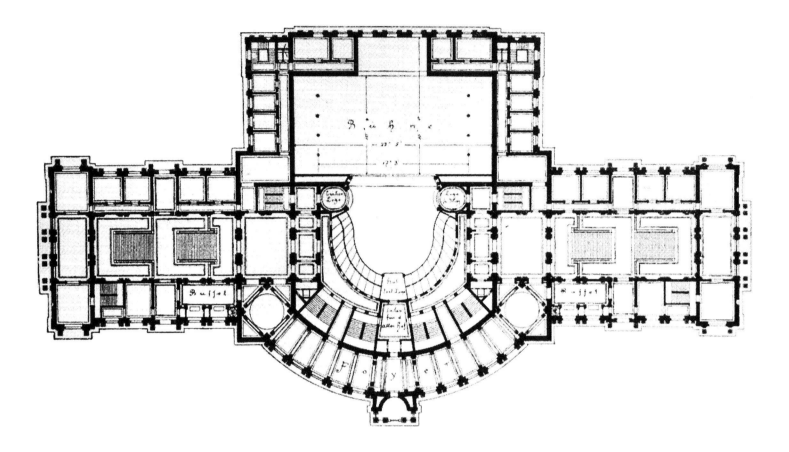

1792 and 1825, of a relatively conventional Georgian town house into what became became his house, office and museum could hardly have been achieved without the use of centralized heating systems.

In those early days heating was almost always considered in combination with ventilation. Public buildings such as theatres presented major ventilation problems, as they still do, and a number of sophisticated designs were realized. There is a long and well-documented history of the difficulty in achieving satisfactory ventilation in the debating chambers of the Palace of Westminster.[8] Figures as eminent as Christopher Wren and Humphry Davy are reported to have attempted solutions. After the destruction of most of the palace in the fire of 1834, a special committee was appointed to 'Consider the best Mode of Warming and Ventilating the New Houses'. Among the witnesses called before the committee was Dr David Boswell Reid, who had trained as a physician and, in 1831, had been elected to the chair of chemistry at Edinburgh University. Reid was commissioned to design the ventilation for Parliament's temporary accommodation and in 1839 was appointed engineering consultant to Charles Barry, winner of the architectural competition for the design of the new Houses of Parliament. The events that followed provide an insight into the difficulties of the relationship between architect and engineer, as the two worlds came together in the realization of probably the most important building project of the time.

Robert Bruegman explains that the working relationship between Reid

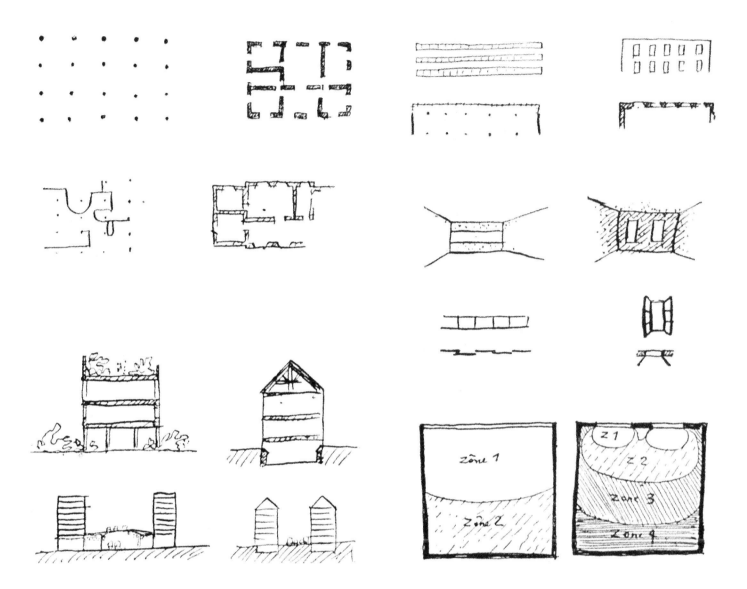

and Barry was not without difficulty. In the early days Reid's demand for a tall ventilation stack was welcomed by Barry, since it gave him the opportunity to add an extra tower to his gothic silhouette. But clashes soon arose when the engineer asked for numerous alterations to Barry's design in order to accommodate his ducts and appliances (fig. 7). In 1852 Reid was dismissed and Barry assumed responsibility for the entire project, including the ventilation systems. These were executed in broad accordance with the principles established by Reid. In spite of this dispute, the completed design demonstrates how the installation of elaborate and space-consuming services could be reconciled with the objectives of high Victorian architects. Barry and Reid both enjoyed greater success with other projects. At the Reform Club (1841) in London's Pall Mall, Barry achieved a remarkable synthesis of architectural expression and technological expertise, this time in the garb of Renaissance Classicism. As John Olley's studies show, an extensive system for warming and ventilation was seamlessly incorporated into the fabric of the gentlemen's club (fig. 8).[9] Olley also gives a detailed account of Reid's apparently happier collaboration with H. L. Elmes in the design of the Greek revival masterpiece of St George's Hall, Liverpool (1841–54).[10] The system installed there has one of the very first forced ventilation systems with steam-driven fans to propel the air through the building (fig. 9). By the middle of the 19th century centralized heating and ventilation systems were widespread in Europe

← fig. 14: Mies van der Rohe, glass skyscraper project, Berlin, 1919; after Hawkes.

→ fig. 15: Le Corbusier, Cité de Refuge, Paris, 1929–33, sealed glass façade; after Le Corbusier, *Oeuvre Complet.*

and North America. Buildings of many types – theatres, hospitals, prisons, exchanges, schools, clubs and the new office buildings – benefited from the potential to create internal environments that were more uniform, predictable and comfortable than any that had gone before. These buildings were designed by many of the greatest architects of the time.

The gap between the engineer and the architect that had developed in post-Revolutionary France – what Giedion described as the 'separation of thought from feeling' – was strongly opposed by Henri Labrouste, a graduate of the Ecole des Beaux-Arts, who in 1830 opened a private atelier in order to promote a 'rationalistic' alternative to both education and practice. Eventually, in his designs for Paris's Bibliothèque Ste.-Geneviève (1843–50) (fig. 10), and then at the Bibliothèque Nationale (1858–68), also in Paris, Labrouste was able to give concrete expression to the possibility of a synthesis of the new technology and architectural language. As Pevsner points out, these achievements undoubtedly influenced Eugène Viollet-le-Duc who, in his *Entretiens* of 1863, argued for the adoption of new methods of manufacture, 'with a view to the adoption of architectural forms adapted to our times' rather than in concealing them 'by an architecture borrowed from other ages'.[11] But, in addition to these innovations in the adoption and expression of constructional techniques, which attracted the attention of the historians of the Modern Movement, Labrouste was at the forefront in applying new environmental tools.

The Bibliothèque Nationale building had not only its poetic, domed reading room and proto-high-tech book stack but also a fully integrated warm-air system (fig. 11).[12] In all probability this contributed as much to the building's radical spatial organization and architectural language as the more visible qualities of its structure.

The German architect, teacher and theoretician Gottfried Semper used advanced systems of heating, ventilation and even cooling in his designs for theatres.[13] There is

evidence that the Dresden Opera House (1841) had an extensive ventilation system and the Hofburg Theatre in Vienna (1874) had a network of collecting, mixing and heating chambers from which air, mixed to an appropriate temperature, was distributed throughout the building (fig. 12). During cold weather stale air was extracted by the natural buoyancy of the warmed air but in summer electrically powered extractor fans were switched on and the incoming air was cooled by being passed over a shallow pond, supplied

from a deep well in the basement. The whole system was operated from an engineer's control room buried in the depths of the building.

Other practical applications of the new means of environmental control were recorded in printed texts. Todd Willmert reports that Soane's library contained copies of *On Conducting Air by Forced Ventilation* (1818) by the Marquis de Chabannes and R. Buchanan's *Practical and Descriptive Essays on the Economy of Fuel and the Management of Heat* (1810). Early textbooks and manuals listed by

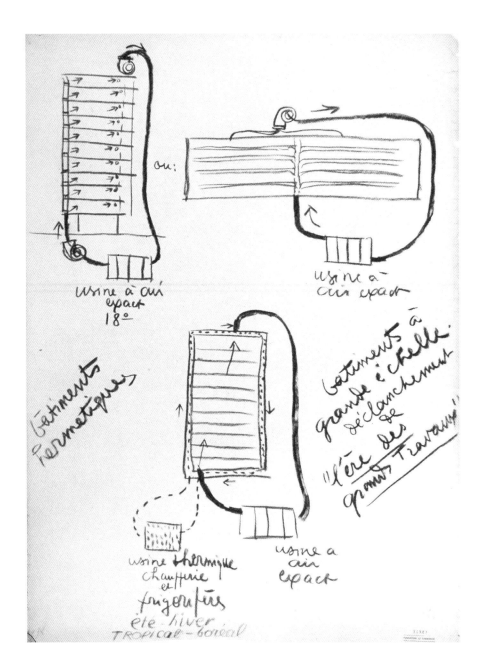

usine à air epact 18°

ou:

usine à air epact

bâtiments hermétiques

bâtiments à grande i-chelle déclanchement de "l'ère des grands Travaux"

usine thermique chaufferie et frigorifères été - hiver TROPICAL - boréal

usine a air epact

←

fig. 16: Le Corbusier, air-conditioning diagram, 1929; after Le Corbusier, *Précisions*.

→

fig. 17: Le Corbusier, Villa Savoye, Poissy, 1929 –31, living room; after Le Corbusier, *Oeuvre Complet*.

Bruegmann include *The Philosophy of Domestic Economy* by Charles Sylvester, which appeared in 1819 and was translated into French in 1824, where it appeared in *Annales de l'Industrie*. One of the most widely available books was Thomas Tredgold's *Principles of Warming and Ventilation* (1824) and Reid published his own *Illustrations of the Theory and Practice of Ventilation* in 1844. In France the first edition of Eugene Peclet's *Etude sur la Chaleur* appeared in 1828, followed by later editions in 1843, 1860 and 1878.

It is clear that environmental engineering had taken its place in everyday building design well before the end of the 19th century. It was common throughout Europe and the USA and was applied in the design of buildings of all types, domestic, public and commercial. Reflecting parallel developments in constructional and structural design, the technological basis of architecture had been fundamentally transformed. David Boswell Reid was emphatic about this when he wrote, 'The great and primary object of architecture is to afford the power of sustaining an artificial atmosphere. Though the invisible air is apt to be forgotten amidst the more obvious attraction of architectural art, still in a practical point of view, the visible structure is only the shell or body of that interior atmosphere without which existence could not be supported.'[14]

This statement is remarkably pertinent to developments in the 20th century, but even at the close of the 19th century architecture maintained contact with principles that had been observed throughout its history. Even

though the utility of buildings was redefined – their use was freer from the constraints of climate than at any other time – and new configurations and dimensions of space had become possible, almost all buildings continued to be daylit. The need to connect the interior to the exterior in order to admit natural light as the principal source of illumination continued to dominate the topography of plans and particularly of cross-sections. Furthermore, and of equal significance, architectural design was still seen as primarily a question of style. This meant that the new technologies, however advanced they might be, were subservient to the fine art of architecture – feeling continued to take priority over thought. In the 20th century, however, all that changed.

The Modern Movement and the new synthesis

In the first decades of the 20th century a radically new conception of architecture emerged. Writing in 1913, the artist Fernand Léger proposed that 'Architecture . . . is emerging from several centuries of false traditionalism and approaching a modern and utilitarian idea of its function.'[15] The implication was that, in becoming 'modern and utilitarian', architecture would be released from the constraints of the styles and would discover new links between its representational and aesthetic goals and its technical aspects. Le Corbusier articulated this when he wrote in the programme of *L'Esprit Nouveau*, 'There is a new spirit: it is a spirit of *construction and synthesis* [authors' emphasis] guided by a clear conception.' [16]

The 'new spirit' was given its clearest expression in *Cinque points d'une architecture nouvelle*, where Le Corbusier and Pierre Jeanneret explicitly proposed the separation of the functions of structure and enclosure, of the replacement of the load-bearing wall, punctured by window openings, with a structural frame and a light, largely transparent enclosing skin (fig. 13).[17] Distinct technical functions are given expression through specific and separate elements of the composition. Perhaps it was at this moment that the idea of the distinct building 'envelope', which has since become commonplace, was born.

In these early statements, the emphasis was almost entirely on the application and expression of the structural and constructional elements of buildings. Mechanical services were almost completely ignored. In Mies van der Rohe's designs for glass skyscrapers for Berlin of 1919 and 1920–21 (fig. 14), the building envelope is reduced to a faceted transparent skin. If these buildings were to be habitable, they would have to be serviced by environmental mechanisms of a sophistication that did not exist at the time. This problem went unremarked. But very soon afterwards Le Corbusier, at the Cité de Refuge, which he designed and built in Paris between 1929 and 1933, proposed the complete integration of the building envelope and environmental services.[18] The idea was to combine a sealed, double-skin wall, the 'mur neutralisant', with a system of mechanical ventilation and heating (fig. 15).

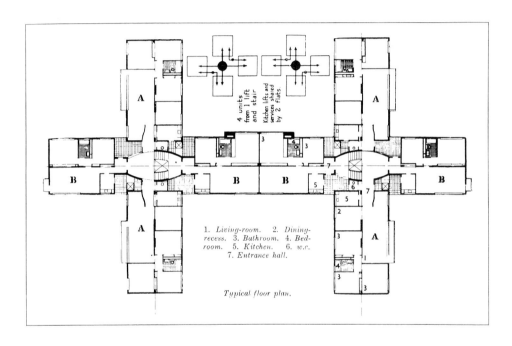

A detailed account of Le Corbusier's intentions can be found in the second of the lectures that he delivered in Buenos Aires in autumn 1929, later published as *Précisions.*[19] A drawing made to illustrate the lecture shows the fundamentals of the system he proposed (fig. 16). Within the sealed skin of the building there is a full air-conditioning system, which supplies and extracts tempered and filtered air. This was to be maintained at 18°C (64°F) with the aim of achieving a universal environmental standard. 'Every country builds its houses in response to its climate. At this moment of general diffusion, of international scientific techniques, I propose: I propose only one house for all countries, the house of *exact breathing* [authors' emphasis].' For reasons of both economy and technical uncertainty this aspect of the Cité de Refuge project was not fully realized. The great south-facing façade was constructed with only a single-glazed skin and, even though the envelope was sealed, the recirculating ventilation system did not supply cooled air.[20]

The significance of the Cité de Refuge is that it is one of the first buildings which, in its intention if not in its realization, fundamentally reordered the elements of architecture to form what became the heart of the Modern Movement's programme. To the demands of the *cinque points* for separation of the functions of support and enclosure Le Corbusier added the logical corollary of mechanical plant as the principal instrument of environmental control and, thereby, established one of the clearest distinctions between the architectures

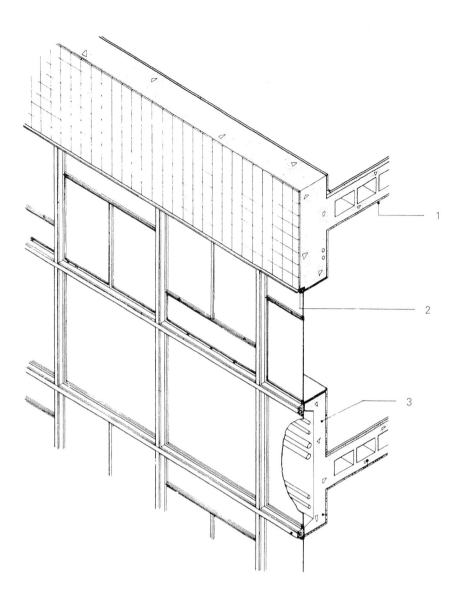

fig. 20: Berthold
Lubetkin, Finsbury
Health Centre,
London,1938, cut-
away isometric
showing integration
of services; after
Allan.

1 Radiant heating
   panels on ceiling
2 Ventilation at head
   of fixed light
3 Reinforced
   concrete walls,
   forming service
   ducts to the
   exterior of the
   building

of the 19th and 20th centuries. The primary agent of climate modification was no longer the massive load-bearing external wall. With its taut, transparent glass façade, the Cité de Refuge was a building whose everyday use depended upon the operation of its mechanical plant. If that were to fail, the building would be uninhabitable. In designing such a building, collaboration between architect and environmental services engineer became essential. At this point, for the first time, the engineer assumed main responsibility for the environmental function of architecture.

Concealed power versus exposed power

Nineteenth-century architects and engineers could incorporate extensive environmental services into the fabric of buildings with hardly any disturbance to the stylistic preoccupations of the time. The bitter dispute between Charles Barry and David Boswell Reid in the design of the Houses of Parliament would not have been unique in the evolving relationship between the professions, but it is likely that there would have been little disagreement about the need to conceal the service systems within the principal spaces of all but the most utilitarian buildings.

The new synthesis of the 20th century meant that the status of service installations within the visible order of architecture was open for reconsideration. If it was now possible to express the difference between structure and enclosure with new-found clarity, it would be equally possible visually to reveal the

fig. 21: Berthold
Lubetkin, Finsbury
Health Centre,
London, 1938,
structural and service
system diagrams;
after Allan.

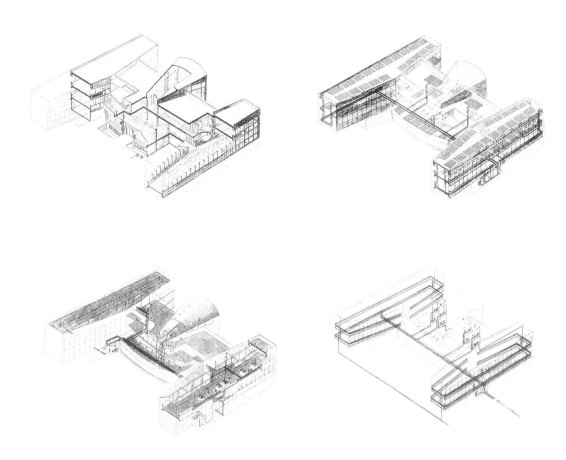

apparatus of heating, ventilation and artificial lighting.

Le Corbusier directly addressed this question in some of his early 'white' villas. In the living room of the Villa Savoye, for example, the purpose-made linear light fitting became a key element of the composition, and no attempt was made to conceal the cast-iron radiators beneath the wide sills of the fenêtre en longueur (fig. 17). At the Cité de Refuge, however, while artificial light fittings were conspicuous in all the main spaces, the elaborate original systems for

heating and ventilation were much more discreetly accommodated (fig. 18). Careful provision was made in the plan for the vertical ducts, but these were not visibly expressed as such.

In *The Architecture of the Well-tempered Environment*, Reyner Banham identifies two approaches to the physical incorporation of plant and services into the fabric of a building: 'concealed power' and 'exposed power'. Many important developments occurred in the technologies of environmental control, particularly in the

mechanisms of refrigeration and air-conditioning, but Banham suggests that the predominant approach to the physical incorporation of services systems in the buildings of the Modern Movement was their concealment rather than their expression.

A particularly sophisticated relationship between engineering and architectural intention was achieved in the 1930s through the collaboration of Berthold Lubetkin and a group of consultant engineers.[21] At the Highpoint apartment buildings in

↓
fig. 22 Le Corbusier,
Unité d'Habitation,
Marseilles, 1947-
1952, sol artificiel;
after Le Corbusier,
Oeuvre Complet.

→
fig. 23: Le Corbusier,
Unité d'Habitation,
Marseilles, 1947-
1952, cheminée de
ventilation; after Le
Corbusier, *Oeuvre
Complet.*

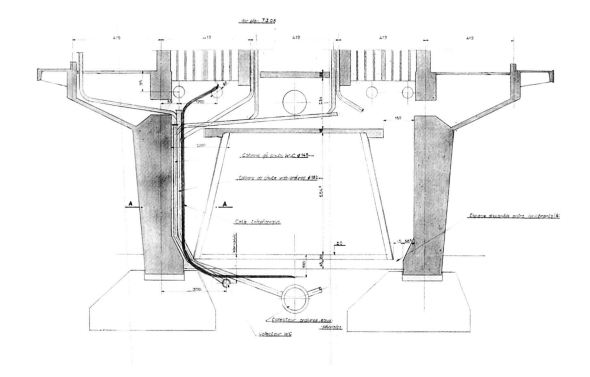

Highgate, north London, and at the Finsbury Health Centre, Lubetkin worked with the structural engineer Ove N. Arup and the services engineers G. N. Haden & Sons. The consultants were involved from the inception of each design, and as a result the architecture, structural design and environmental services achieved a high degree of integration.

The environmental emphasis at Highpoint was on the Modernist virtues of natural light and fresh air, but, in addition to large windows and planning for cross-ventilation, the apartments were equipped with concealed radiant ceiling heating providing, as Lubetkin stated, 'pleasant heat with no draughts. Air not stuffy.' All the plumbing was located in accessible ducts, as were the extensive electrical services (fig. 19). The Finsbury Health Centre had a more demanding environmental programme than Highpoint, and the integration of the services systems within the structure was realized in total accord with the functional and architectural intentions. Four distinct but interconnected technical systems were defined: the construction system, the heating system, the electrical system and the plumbing system (fig. 20). The primary service runs for each system were located within a void formed between the main structural beams and the curtain walling. From this position they were fed into the building (fig. 21).

The development of the independent structural frame, curtain wall and suspended ceiling as the kit from which buildings for many purposes could be made allowed the concealment of extensive plant in

deep ceiling voids. While this kit-of-parts became the 'vernacular architecture' of corporate 20th-century culture, it has its origins in the works of Mies van der Rohe. But, as Kenneth Frampton shows in *Studies in Tectonic Culture*, the tectonic was, for Mies, not an end in itself, but the instrument through which he might seek 'the embodiment of the spirit in the banality of the real'.[22] The suspended ceiling was not merely a convenient covering for the service mechanisms in the void above but became a representation of 'abstract materiality'

in contradiction of the actual materiality of his structures and the natural materials of his floors. This was further sustained by Mies's open embrace of the idea of concealed power. Frampton writes, 'Mies recognised modern technology as a dichotomous destiny that was at once both destroyer and provider. He saw it as the apocalyptic demiurge of the new era and as the inescapable matrix of the modern world.'

If you look at the collage of the interior of the project for a Museum for a Small City (1943), you may deduce

that the shadowless uniformity of the visual field is the product of an even distribution of artificial illumination issuing from a diffusing ceiling. This is intended not as a night-time substitute for natural light but as the primary light source at all times of day or night. The heating also issues, silently and continuously, from concealed outlets in the ceiling and, perhaps, from other elements of the building fabric. Exactly this effect was anticipated in the silk exhibition that Mies designed in collaboration with Lily Reich at the German section of the Barcelona International

↓
fig. 24: Marco
Zanusso, Olivetti
Factory, Argentina,
1964, cut-away
perspective showing
relation of structure
and mechanical plant;
after Banham.

1 Exposed end of
  hollow concrete
  beam
2 Main roof structure
3 Air conditioner unit
  attached to end of
  hollow-beam duct
4 Monitor lights
  in roof

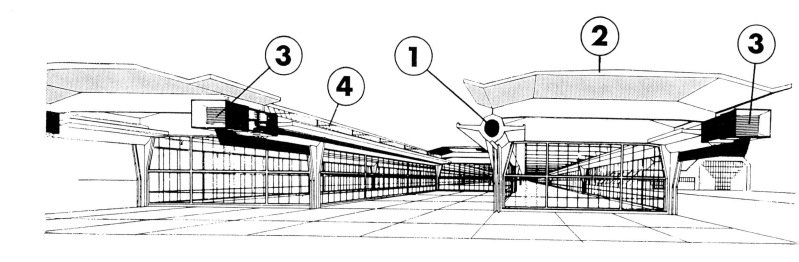

Exposition in 1929. In Mies's built projects during his mature period from the early 1940s, it can be seen how this environmental complement to his tectonic visions was brought to masterly realization. At the IIT campus in Chicago, particularly in the central buildings such as Crown Hall (1956), at the National Gallery in Berlin (1958) and, perhaps most influential of all, at the Seagram Building in New York (1958), this vision of the seamless, imperceptible, but 'ideal' environment, invisibly supplied, is brought to complete realization.

Banham argues that the invisibly serviced glass enclosure satisfied a primary aesthetic objective of the Modern Movement. On the other hand, it contradicted the 'moral imperative' that the functions and elements of a building should be given honest expression. In the years after the Second World War this position was challenged by designs such as Le Corbusier's Unité d'Habitation at Marseilles. There the extensive services networks were gathered and organized sectionally in the sol artificiel, poised over the piloti

(fig. 22), and the air extract ducts were given sculptural form in the playful composition of the roof terrace (fig. 23). Other architects began to explore ways to express the new relationship between structure and services. Banham illustrates Marco Zanusso's Olivetti Factory in Argentina (1964), with its exposed air-conditioning units plugged directly into hollow tubular roof beams (fig. 24). Here the extensive roof of the single-storey building becomes a combined structural and environmental canopy over the production space. In Rome,

fig. 25: Franco Albini,
Rinascente department
store, Rome, 1961, cut-
away axonometric
showing services ducts
integrated into façade;
after Banham.

1 Plant room in roof
2 Vertical distribution duct
3 Precast cladding
4 External steel framing
5 Distribution duct to
   sales space

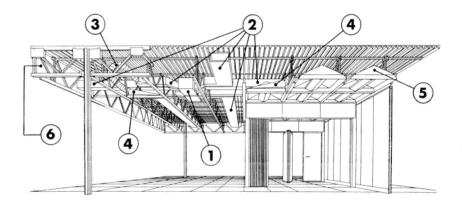
fig. 26: SCSD school
prototype, 1966;
after Banham.

1 Mixing boxes for
  air from conditioner
  on roof
2 Rigid distribution ducts
3 Flexible distribution
  ducts
4 Ceiling outlets
5 Lighting system
6 Roof space acting as
  return air plenum

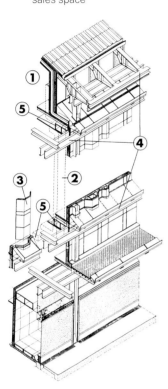

Franco Albini designed a modern palazzo for the department store La Rinascente (1961), in which the service systems are carried in voids formed within the precast concrete cladding, all supported on an exposed steel structure (fig. 25).[23]

In the USA during this period the idea of rationalized construction and the exploitation of mechanical technology in environmental design was given its most utilitarian and in some respects most influential expression in the Schools Construction System Development (SCSD) programme.[24] Evolving from a research project carried out under the direction of Ezra Ehrenkrantz at Stanford University, the idea of the system was to construct a light steel roof structure over a deep-plan space within which internal partitions could be placed to provide many alternative arrangements, all serviced by adjustable artificial lighting and air-conditioning supplies. The image of the rooftop air-conditioning unit being delivered by helicopter (fig. 26) spoke loudly of the triumph of technology over nature, as the fully artificial environment replaced the benign climate of California.

The most influential building of this time was almost certainly Louis Kahn's Richards Memorial Laboratories in Philadelphia, completed in 1961 (fig. 27). 'I do not like ducts, I do not like pipes,' said Kahn. 'I hate them really thoroughly, but because I hate them so thoroughly, I feel that they have to be given their place. If I just hated them and took no care, I think that they would invade the building and completely destroy it. I want to correct

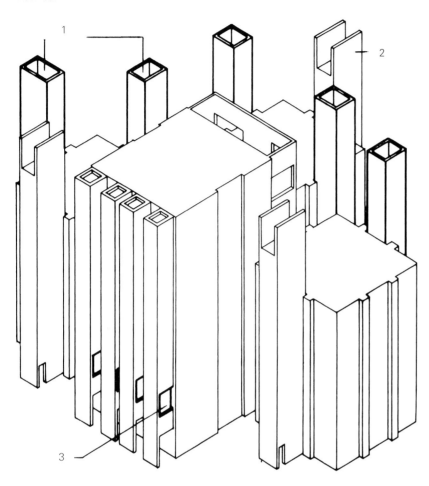

fig. 27: Louis Kahn, Richards Memorial Laboratories, Philadelphia, 1961, axonometric showing service towers; after Hawkes.

(1) Service towers; (2) Stair tower; (3) Air intakes.

any notion you may have that I am in love with that kind of thing.'[25] Kahn issued this cri de coeur after the completion of the Richards building. Along with his distinction between 'served' and 'servant' spaces, this building provoked a new phase in the approach to the deliberate exposure of service systems, but it was the specific nature of the laboratory building, with service systems far more extensive than those of most other building types, that led Kahn to his particular and, in many ways, radical solution. In all his later designs, whether for art museums or centres of government, however carefully he organized the distribution of services in relation to space and structure, the approach was conceived in strict observance of the implications of the programme. Technical display for its own sake was anathema to Kahn, as attested by the subtle integration and concealment of the services installations at the Kimbell Art Museum at Fort Worth (1972) (fig. 28) and the Mellon Center for British Art at New Haven (1974) (fig. 29).

In a line that continues to the present day, the influence of the Richards building can be traced to many later designs. Perhaps the clearest early example of influence may be seen in the early works of the 'high-tech' school in the 1970s.[26] Although they adopt a completely different approach to questions of materiality and representation from that of Kahn, both the Pompidou Centre (Renzo Piano and Richard Rogers, 1977) (fig. 30) and the Lloyds Building (Richard Rogers, 1984) (fig. 31) owe a clear debt to Kahn in their

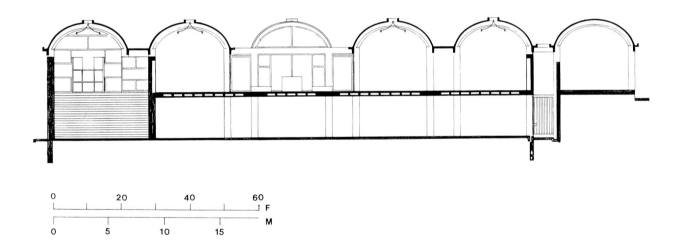

emphatic location and expression of mechanical plant as 'servant' space relative to the 'served' enclosure.

In the 1980s this lineage was challenged, albeit briefly, by the emergence of architectural Postmodernism.[27] At the heart of this movement, in most of its various and varied manifestations, was the rejection of the kind of 'objectivity' and 'instrumentality' that had informed the development of architecture, in theory and practice, through much of the 20th century. With its preoccupation with new kinds of interpretation, historicism and, as Frampton put it, the scenographic over the tectonic,[28] questions of environmental control and of the systematic organization of services installations received little attention in Postmodern theory. But, as is so often the case in architecture, buildings are as revealing as theory.

The Postmodern environment can be characterized by Robert Venturi's design for the Sainsbury Wing at the National Gallery in London, completed in 1991 (fig. 32).[29] In the modern picture gallery strict control of lighting and air quality are crucial for the safe display and conservation of works of art. In addressing this need, Venturi's design began, not with Modernist analysis, but with reference to what he describes as 'the body of traditional practice'. The picture galleries in the Sainsbury Wing were modelled on John Soane's Dulwich Picture Gallery. The two buildings have the same arrangement of clerestorey windows providing even and controlled illumination of the walls and pictures, but in Venturi's building all is not what it seems.

Beyond the clerestorey, which is glazed with etched glass, there is a further layer of rooftop structure and enclosure. This is an elaborate mechanism of environmental control, in which banks of adjustable louvres and fluorescent lamps operate in concert to regulate the amount of light that enters the galleries. This creates an illusion of constant natural light in the galleries, but for much of the time, even in daytime, the light source is artificial. This is pure environmental scenography; the pictures are lit individually and precisely by spotlamps mounted in the ceiling.

The building is fully air-conditioned, a necessary requirement of the modern urban art museum, but artifice rather than expression of the extensive installation is again at work. Its cellular plan gives the impression of massive, load-bearing construction – the openings between rooms are lined with solid stone architraves and this continues as a deep skirting – but the building is actually a steel-framed construction and the thick walls are made of plasterboard supported on a light steel framing system, providing plenty of voids in which the air-conditioning ducts can be concealed.

So, after the Modern Movement had attempted to define clear geometrical and functional relationships between, space, construction and environmental systems, at the end of the 20th century architects demonstrated that all the complexity of the controlled environment could be organized in the service of the picturesque. The delivery of 'concealed power' resumed its subservient position in the architectural hierarchy.

fig. 30: Renzo Piano and Richard Rogers, Pompidou Centre, Paris, 1977, east 'service' façade.

fig. 29: Louis Kahn, Mellon Center for British Art, New Haven, 1974, interior of picture gallery.

The evolving envelope

In the 1930s Le Corbusier added a new element to the apparatus of modern architecture with his invention of the brise-soleil. It first appeared in his project for an apartment building in Algiers in which the south and west façades were shaded by a concrete 'egg-crate' structure. The most celebrated early installation was in the design of the Ministry of Education building in Rio de Janeiro (1936–45) (fig. 33), a collaboration with Lucio Costa, where the brise-soleil were added to the standard repertoire of the cinque points, 'columns, glass façades, independent framework, roof garden, etc.'[30] This signalled the beginning of a process by which the external envelope of the modern building has become progressively more complex in the service of environmental control.

Writing in 1962, Alan Colquhoun pointed out that, by the mid 20th century, the clarity of the cinque points on the separation of structure and enclosure had been replaced in many buildings by a revival of interest in heavy and traditional methods of construction: 'It is as if the urge to create the world anew by means of structures which had the lightness and tenuousness of pure thought had given way to the desire to create solid hideouts of the human spirit in a world of uncertainty and change, each one a microcosm of an ideal world.'[31]

The late buildings of Louis Kahn exemplify this trend. The Richards Laboratory, the Kimbell Art Museum and the Mellon Center all retain a clearly articulated distinction between frame and envelope, but in every case the envelope combines areas of solid

fig. 31: Richard
Rogers, Lloyds
Building, London,
1984.

and void in proportions appropriate to the function of the building. In Kahn's first project outside the USA – the unbuilt design for the US consulate in Luanda, Angola (1959–61) (fig. 34) – he responded to the equatorial climate by constructing a deeply layered envelope with unglazed screens standing in front of deeply recessed windows and by surmounting the 'rain roof' with a structurally independent 'sun roof' to provide shade and promote natural ventilation. In the library at Philips Academy, Exeter, New Hampshire (1965–71) (fig.

35), where climate was less of a challenge, the entire envelope was enclosed, but distinct environmental zones were established within the plan's concentric territories. Readers sit in the brick-built, daylit perimeter, where aedicular desks are located within the oak window frames, and books, which are more environmentally sensitive than readers, are placed in the thermally massive *in-situ* concrete core, where it is easier to maintain a stable environment.

These projects helped to reassert the environmental function of a

building's external envelope, whereby it acts as a mediator, a 'filter', between internal and external climates. Although the highly serviced glass box continues to exert its appeal, the potential of the more complex, environmentally considered façade is explored increasingly often in contemporary designs. A discipline has emerged in which arbitrary form-making and stylism have no place but which opens up rich possibilities for the development of architectural language. In asserting the authority of the tectonic in architecture, Kenneth

←
fig. 32: Robert Venturi, Sainsbury Wing, National Gallery, London, 1991; after Hawkes.

Frampton has argued that 'the tectonic does not necessarily favour any particular style'.[32] The same may be said of environmental design principles, which are neither formally nor stylistically determinate; good architects and engineers may adapt them creatively to the programme, context, economy and culture of each project. The buildings described in detail later in this book illustrate the diversity and sophistication of the modern environmental envelope.

Natural versus mechanical energy
Pointing to the ever-accelerating consumption of mineral reserves, as industrialization provided more and more tools for an increasingly urbanized world, Derry and Williams argued that a crucial change had taken place in Western man's relationship with natural resources in the period between 1750 and 1900.[33] In the field of architecture and building, one of the central themes during this period was the conversion of the energy stored in fossil fuels to power consumed in devices for

environmental control. This paradigm survived the arrival of architectural Modernism and was given impetus by the emergence of the idea of an 'International Style' in which, as Le Corbusier put it in *Précisions*, 'international scientific techniques [allow us] to propose only one house for all countries'. Building trends throughout the 20th century confirmed the potency of this idea. The air-conditioned glass skyscraper has become that 'one house for all countries', providing international business and recreation interests with

fig. 33: Le Corbusier
and Lucio Costa,
Ministry of
Education, Rio de
Janeiro, 1936–45.

a uniform, controlled internal environment wherever they may be. In the last quarter of the 20th century, however, the assumption that the march of technological progress would, and should, continue indefinitely was seriously questioned – first by a growing awareness of the limits of the earth's fossil-fuel resources, and then by the apprehension that their continued consumption at established rates was having an irreversibly destructive effect on the world's climate. A new perspective on the objectives and

methods of environmental control in buildings emerged, which focuses on ways of reducing demand for non-renewable sources of energy and mechanical power and explores ways in which they might be replaced by renewable natural resources.

The environmental strategy applied in architecture, whether consciously or unconsciously, before the Industrial Revolution may be described in terms of the 'Vitruvian model' (fig. 36).[34] According to this model, 'architecture', as a portmanteau term embracing all elements of building, is represented

as the mediation between the unpredictable climate and the more stable conditions necessary to sustain the functions of human society.

In *Design with Climate*, one of the 20th century's most important books about the relationship between climate and architecture, Victor Olgyay proposed a model of 'interlocking fields of climate balance' (fig. 37) which explicitly extends the Vitruvian model by distinguishing between architecture (the static organization and fabric of a building) and the new element, technology

fig. 34: Louis Kahn,
Project for US Consulate,
Luanda, Angola, 1959–61,
cut-away axonometric
showing environmentally
layered envelope.

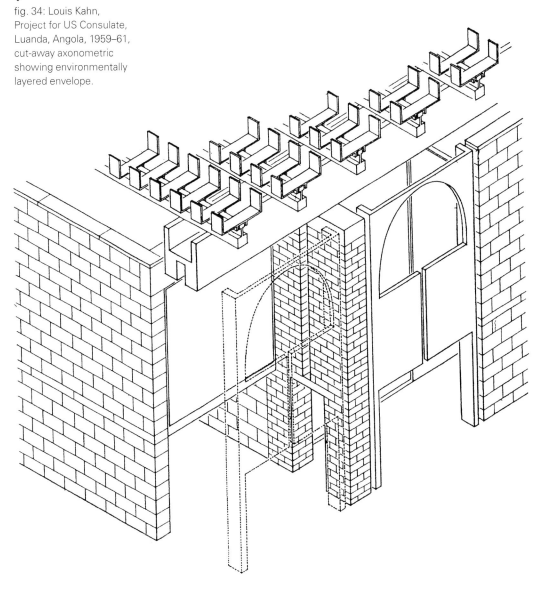

(mechanical services), in the process of environmental control.[35] This distinction describes the basis of almost all contemporary environmental design in architecture and suggests the primacy of the collaboration between architect and engineer. But, writing in 1963, Olgyay was constructing a framework that more precisely represented the balance between the environmental functions of architecture and technology. In an elegantly simple diagram related to the 'interlocking fields' model and called 'flattening the curve' (fig. 38), Olgyay defined the stages by which wide variations of climate – in this instance of temperature – might be progressively modified. In this he distinguishes between the roles of 'microclimatology', 'climate balance of the structure' and, finally, 'mechanical heating or cooling'. The point of the exercise was to show how manipulation of the first two of these variables might significantly reduce the demands placed upon the mechanical plant. In effect this is an argument for the whole building, its architecture and its technology, to be conceived as a system of complementary and interlocking parts.

Olgyay's book is one of the key documents in the development of an environmentally friendly approach to architecture. In it he uses the term 'bioclimatic architecture' to describe designs that set out to work with rather than against nature. Much of the pioneering work in bioclimatic architecture was in designs for small dwellings, in most cases using the techniques of 'passive solar' design to meet some, if not all, the space-

fig. 35: Louis Kahn,
Library, Philips
Academy, Exeter,
New Hampshire,
1965–72.

fig. 36: The 'Vitruvian'
model of environmental
design; after Hawkes.

fig. 37: 'Interlocking
fields of climate balance',
after Victor Olgyay, 1963;
after Olgyay.

fig. 38: 'Flattening the
curve', after Victor Olgyay,
1963; after Olgyay.
1 Environmental condition
2 Microclimatology
3 Climate balance of
   structure
4 Mechanical heating or
   cooling

fig. 39: Steve Baer House,
New Mexico; after
Steadman.

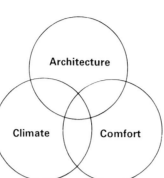

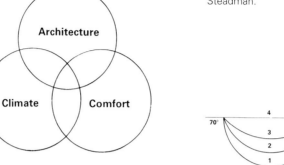

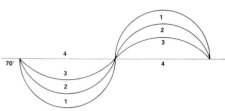

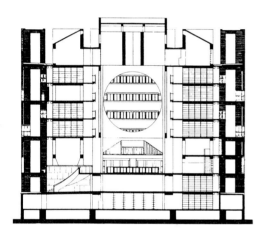

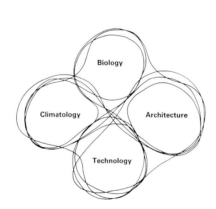

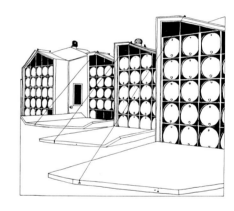

heating requirements (fig. 39).[36] Other projects sought the more ambitious goal of 'autonomy' (fig. 40), in which all a dwelling's servicing needs could be met without dependence on mains services of any kind.[37] Such ventures made it possible to test new ideas before they gradually found their way into the design of larger buildings. By the late 1980s there was an increasing number of designs for various building types in which some of these lessons were being effectively applied.[38] Norman Foster's Lycée Polyvalent at Fréjus in the south of France (1991–93)

(fig. 41) exhibits, in its array of brise-soleil, the respect for orientation that is one of the cornerstones of bioclimatic design. The concrete structure provides thermal mass to moderate extremes of temperature and the cross-section is manipulated to promote controllable natural ventilation. In their design for the Queen's Building at De Montfort University at Leicester in the English Midlands (1989–93) (fig. 42), Short Ford & Associates combined references to the brick tradition of English architecture with a powerful

expression of the terminals of the building's natural ventilation stacks, although the impact of this gesture was compromised by the building's curious appropriation of quasi-Victorian stylism. In Austria, Thomas Herzog reinterpreted the idea of the 'crystal palace' in his design for a congress and exhibition hall at Linz (1986–94) (fig. 43). The complex layering of glazing and louvres achieves a high level of natural light in the hall without the disadvantage of uncontrollable solar-heat gains. The form of the arched roof also promotes

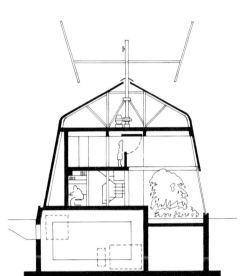

natural ventilation of the vast space.

The Malaysian architect Ken Yeang has developed his own interpretation of bioclimatic design.[39] His bioclimatic skyscraper projects in South-east Asia have brought a systematic approach to the design of the building envelope to bear on the extreme climate of that region. The Menara Mesiniaga office building in Selangor, Malaysia (1989–92) (fig. 44) fuses understanding of environmental principles with late 20th-century structural and material technologies.

A taxonomy of environmental architecture

The recent history of architecture has seen the development of a new and more sophisticated synthesis and collaboration between leading architectural and engineering practices. Numerous developments in the technology of building have greatly expanded the tectonic and environmental repertoire and, as a consequence, the scope of environmental design. Contemporary practice exhibits a greater diversity of approach than ever before.

As we have tried to show in our outline of the environmental history of architecture since the 18th century, the basis of this diversity rests on the relationship between the environmental function of form and fabric of a building and its mechanical service systems. Before the development of mechanical service systems it was form and fabric that, through their configuration and materiality, provided a permeable and, often, highly effective boundary between the external climate and the internal environment – the Vitruvian model.

↓
fig. 42: Short Ford,
Queen's Building, De
Montfort University,
Leicester, UK,
1989–93; after
Hawkes.

↓
fig. 43: Thomas
Herzog, Congress
and Exhibition Hall,
Linz, Austria,
1986–94; after
Herzog.

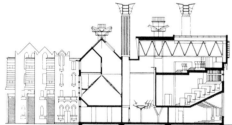

As service systems developed in the 19th and 20th centuries, they added to the environmental scope of form and fabric and, in the process, produced higher and more predictable standards of comfort. With the full apparatus of modern mechanical servicing – plant for heating, cooling, ventilating, lighting – and with the achievement of the sealed envelope, it became possible to deliver a controlled, and by implication 'perfect', artificial environment within a building.

The enormous diversity of present-day environmental design practice is based on alternative interpretations and adaptations of this history. Some designs continue to work with a combination of form and fabric operating in a calculated relationship with mechanical systems. Others separate the external and internal climates with a sealed enclosure and apply mechanical services as the main providers of the internal environment. These two *modes* of environmental control have been defined as, respectively, the *selective* and the *exclusive*.[40]

This classification distinguishes between designs that, in *selective* mode, *selectively* accommodate and filter the ambient environment as their primary strategy and those that, in *exclusive* mode, configure and construct the building enclosure to achieve maximum *exclusion* of the external climate in order to minimize the demands placed on environmental plant. Such a distinction broadly characterizes the predominant environmental options, but the richness and complexity of modern practice demands a more refined taxonomy.

To structure the discussion of the 'critical studies' that follow we

↓
fig. 44: Ken Yeang,
Menara Mesiniaga,
Selangor, Malaysia,
1989–92; after
Powell.

↓
fig. 45: A taxonomy
of environmental
architecture and
engineering.

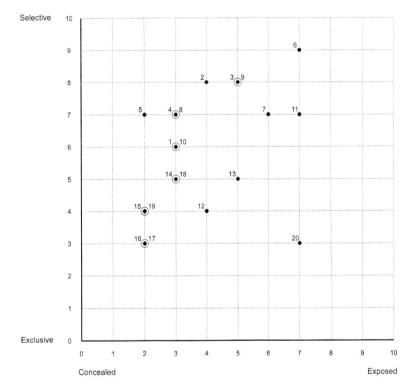

propose a descriptive scheme that extends the distinction between *selective* and *exclusive* by taking note of the way in which the environmental systems of a building are, in a key distinction drawn by Banham, either *concealed* or *exposed*.

In combination, these factors provide a means of characterizing the environmental strategy of a building. A simple graphic representation is given at fig. 45. Each of the buildings has been given a 'score' between 0 and 10 on the two axes, *selective/ exclusive* and *concealed/exposed*

and, on this basis, is located on the 'solution space' of the diagram. The order in which the projects appear in the book has been used to identify the buildings on the graph:

1 Offices for Apicorp
2 Eastgate
3 Arup Campus
4 Howlands Farm Student Housing
5 Marzahn Low-Energy Apartment Building
6 BedZED Sustainable Development
7 Mont Cenis Training Centre
8 Study Centre, Darwin College

9 Jubilee Campus, University of Nottingham
10 Cultural Centre
11 Carmel Mountain Ranch Public Library
12 Helicon Building
13 Villa VPRO Offices
14 Beyeler Foundation Museum
15 Byzantine Fresco Chapel Museum
16 Museum of Contemporary Art
17 Walsall Art Museum
18 Tate Modern
19 Portuguese Pavilion
20 Velodrome

The Selective Mode

Offices for Apicorp
DEGW
Al Khobar, Saudi Arabia
2000

→
The building envelope
as climatic filter:
model of the Apicorp
project.

Any review of Middle Eastern modern architecture would reveal a body of work that has relied largely on the borrowing of ideas from other, mainly Western cultures. This penchant for cut-and-paste architecture has almost obliterated the best traditions of the regional architecture that had evolved in response to climate and culture. The energy-guzzling glass towers and malls of the temperate Western climates seem even more absurd when transported to hot arid zones.

The Arab Petroleum Investments Corporation (APICORP) is an investment company based at Al Khobar in Saudi Arabia. The company was established in 1975 by the governments of the member states of OPEC. In 1995, when the company needed a new headquarters, an international competition was held to find a suitable design. The brief stipulated that the new building 'should respect the existing context and allude to traditional Arab architecture without resorting to

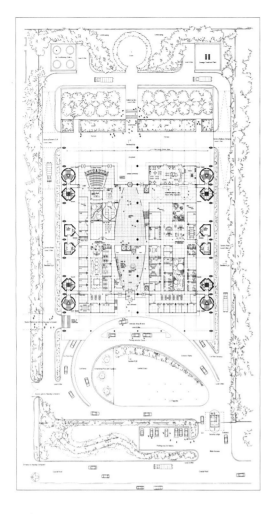

↑
Site plan

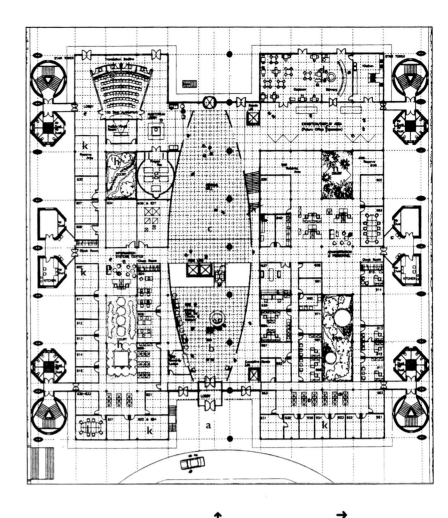

↑
Ground-floor plan.

→
Model at design
stage.

pastiche'.[1] The six ranked
competition entries were designs by
Harry Seidler, Henning Larsen, HOK
International, Fitzroy Robinson, Alberts
& Van Hunt, and DEGW.

Site
The site is next to the company's
existing housing compound, designed
in the late 1970s by Studio Nervi,
which consists of two monumental
curved apartment blocks that lock
together around a central courtyard.
The blocks are stepped back in section
from the courtyard, providing shaded
balconies, but little shelter is provided
in the large central courtyard, and it is
difficult to imagine any architecture
less responsive in form to the location
and local climate.

The competitors' responses to the
brief are worth comparing. They
varied from attempts to harmonize
with the existing formal language of
Nervi (Seidler Associates) to
'grandiose external expression'
(Fitzroy Robinson and HOK
International) and exercises in
singular 'self-contemplation'.[2]

Only two entries seemed to respond
to place and climate, but Henning
Larsen's concept was regarded as
lacking respect for Apicorp's corporate
identity and programming
requirements, while DEGW's
proposals resolved issues of
corporate identity, organizational
needs and response to regional
climate and place, if not to the
immediate context – and the company
emerged as a clear winner.

Located on the Gulf coast of Saudi
Arabia, the site is a challenge for
designers of the modern workplace.
Daytime temperatures rise above 40°C
(104°F) for six to seven months of the
year. Relative humidity is also high –
frequently 70 per cent, and sometimes
as high as 90 per cent. The coastal
location makes for a heavily saline
atmosphere that is potentially
corrosive not only to many metallic
building materials but also to
reinforced-concrete structures unless
they are detailed carefully and
protected. From October to April,
temperatures fall to a mean of
20–30°C (68–86°F). At night,
temperatures can fall to below 10°C
(50°F). Although annual average
rainfall is not high, occasional
rainstorms can be heavy because of
the coastal location.

Building form and organization
The architectural response to the
demands of site, context and
organization is simple and elegant. A
massive sinusoidal roof is employed

as a sheltering element. It is designed to act as a sunshade and also as an all-embracing form for the concept of 'office as village'. DEGW have a long and notable track record in office-building research and design. Francis Duffy, one of the founders of DEGW, presented a doctoral thesis on office organizations at Princeton in 1974 [3] and in 1976 the DEGW book *Planning Office Space* was published. [4] These publications established DEGW's identity as a practice whose approach to office design was founded on matching building and organizational characteristics, post-occupancy evaluation, space budgeting and participating briefing. Design proposals and built reality are both tested through research.

DEGW drew on this tradition in the design for Apicorp. In recognition that the client needed a building that

would provide the potential for a range of different kinds of workplace, the 'office as village' was organized around a series of courtyards. Essentially, Apicorp is conceived as a conventional shell-and-core building but subtly manipulated to suit programme and place. The large central elliptical courtyard is surrounded by four subsidiary courtyards flanked by perimeter 'outboard' service towers, all sheltering under the great roof canopy. These cores are expressed externally as free-standing silos and they articulate the external wall. Flanked by two three-storey office wings, the toplit central courtyard at the heart of the building contains a public reception area at the front and access to auditorium, prayer room and refectory at the rear. Above ground floor the elliptical courtyard

space is crossed by a bridge connecting the two office wings. The wings are not symmetrical: one floor plate is 24m (79ft) wide and the other is 18m (59ft), and these are effectively narrowed by the penetration of the secondary courtyards. Although such a variety of floor plates offers a high degree of workspace flexibility, the initial need of the client is for mainly cellular spaces.

Organizationally Apicorp is a world away from the current norm of northern European offices, with their 'hot desking', 'romp' anywhere, 'home base' mix of space that is capable of 'overnight' change, but Apicorp's cells can also be transformed when required. The floor-plate depth combines with the planning grid to enable a range of workplace configurations. At occupation the building is 90 per cent cellular but it

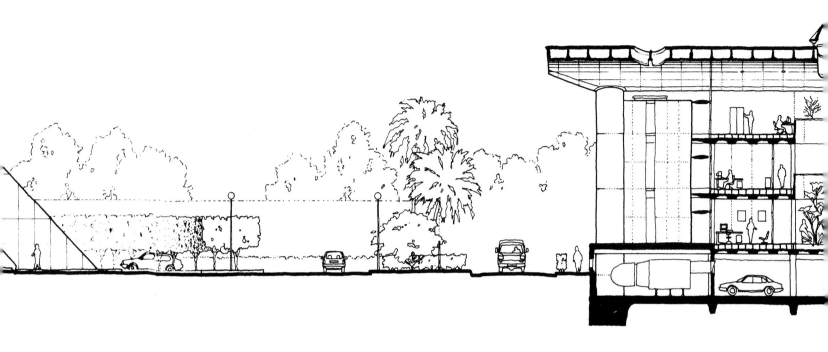

has been designed to promote social interaction. As the social heart of the building, the central courtyard is a key component in this design. The whole building sits on a podium above an underground car park.

Structure and construction

Apicorp's shell, structure, services and scenery are based on DEGW's preferred office-planning module of 1.5m by 1.5m (5ft by 5ft). The structure consists of a primary and secondary structural grid, the primary element of which is the great barrel-vaulted roof supported on gigantic elliptical columns on the north and south perimeters placed at 9m (30ft) centres. The full span of 72m (236ft) from perimeter column to perimeter column is divided by a central column placed asymetrically in the elliptical courtyard. The 36m (118ft) span is

further subdivided by secondary columns at 6m (20ft) centres, and the resulting overall 9m by 6m (30ft by 20ft) structural grid supports the planning and constructional module.

The 9m (30ft) span from column to column is covered at roof level by ribbed precast-concrete vaults supported on primary *in-situ* concrete beams. Profiled metal decking has been laid over these and a layer of in-situ concrete poured over this insulation and placed on top of the concrete. Ceramic tiles have been laid as an external finish. As well as enhancing Apicorp's corporate identity (a primary requirement of the competition brief), the roof also plays a central role in the building's environmental control. In addition to providing solar shading and reflection, layered roof construction, in conjunction with the large hollow

columns, forms part of the distribution system for ventilation to the courtyard. The three floors of office space are supported on a waffle *in-situ* concrete slab. The whole floor zone is 800mm (32in) deep and incorporates a raised floor; clear floor-to-ceiling height in the offices is 3m (10ft) with a structural floor-to-floor height of 3.8m (12ft). This extends to 5.2m (17ft) on the floor where the barrel vault is exposed.

The traditional elements of the international commercial façade – full-height glazing and in-board perimeter columns – have been eschewed in favour of a system that meets local environmental demands. Solid spandrels, clad in local marble and fixed flush with the double-glazed window units, provide thermal mass and privacy. The glazing pattern is designed to reflect Arabic tiling and

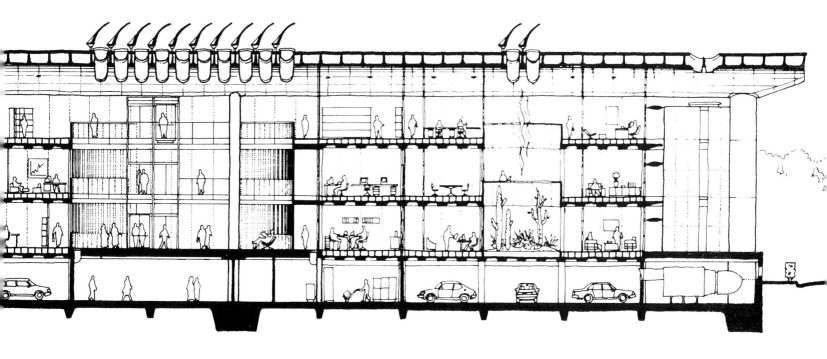

screens. A chequer-plate pattern of smaller windows is placed at eye level, and larger windows are positioned at a higher level to throw light deeper into the plan and add reflected light from the ceilings. The vertical surfaces of walls and windows are protected from direct sun by the over-sailing roof and louvred screens on the east and west façades.

Energy and environment

Thermal mass is traditionally used to modify climate in hot arid zones, but the maritime nature of the site limited the effectiveness of this traditional strategy for Apicorp's new headquarters. Arup calculated that, although there is some potential for free night cooling between October and May (by drawing cool night air through the building), the fan energy needed to push the air through

the filtration and heat-recovery equipment exceeded energy savings through passive cooling because of high air resistance.

The environmental strategy was therefore based on careful integration and balance between building services and structures and fabric. The effects of roof shade and filtered daylight reduce energy demands for heating and cooling. The environmental strategy, even without the benefit of passive cooling, demonstrates a 60 per cent reduction in annual energy consumption compared with a typical North American office.

All the courtyards are daylit through the roof. Rooflights, elliptical on plan, are cut into the barrel vaults over the central and subsidiary courtyards. Direct solar gains are prevented by elegantly designed shades. High sun

angles can make rooflighting design very difficult, and at Al Khobar during the summer the sun reaches an angle of 81 degrees from the horizon – but, even though the sun can be virtually overhead, the depth of the roof construction combined with the external screening admits only first or second reflections.

The deep-plan building is divided into two environmental zones. Its perimeter is subject to the modified effects of the external climate; fluctuations in room loads are dealt with by fan-coil units located in the raised floor. In the more stable zones deeper in the plan, a conventional displacement ventilation system operates. The raised floor acts as a plenum for supply air and low-velocity floor outlets provide delivery. The double-skin roof also forms part of the building's mechanized ventilation

 Building façade at entry: day (top) and night (bottom).

↑ A construction shot, clearly showing the sinusoidal roof.

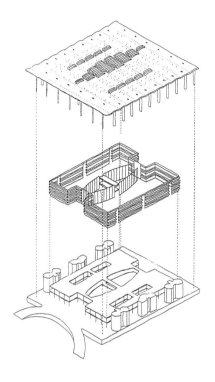

system: air rises from floor level and
enters the hollow roof structure;
exhaust air is drawn through the void
and down vertical ducts in the large
hollow columns to the plant rooms in
the basement plinth. In summer,
exhaust air is dumped into the
enclosed car park to aid cooling.

Conclusion

The new Apicorp headquarters
exemplifies a new regional
architecture that responds to the
demands of climate in a traditional
way but is also based on selective
borrowing from other cultures. In the
development of modern architecture
in the Middle East, the borrowing of
ideas has sometimes been reduced to
the cloning of images but, as Khaled
Asfour suggests, 'Borrowed ideas do
interact with different circumstances
on transfer, giving birth to

interpretations so particular (and so
private) to the new settings that
outcomes become self-
sustainable.... Once a tradition is
established in this field, borrowing
ideas becomes an advantage, not a
burden on design quality.' [5]

It may be too soon to see benefits
from the combination of borrowing
and the exploitation of local energy
resources, but Apicorp's design team
have suggested how these resources
used in conjunction with intelligent
architectural form may lead to a new
discourse among those who practise
architecture in the Middle East.

↑
Early design sketches
of central court.

Eastgate
Pearce Partnership
Harare, Zimbabwe
1996

→
The roof of the building is a complex of environmental devices. This detailed view shows the ensemble of glazed canopy over the atrium, the ventilation chimneys for the offices and solar collectors that supply hot water to the building.

At the beginning of a new millennium the question of globalism versus regionalism has assumed great significance in the political, economic, social and cultural debate. It can be argued that, in some respects, architecture led the way towards global culture. The image of the glass skyscraper was proposed in Mies van der Rohe's Berlin projects of 1919 and 1922. Le Corbusier's declaration –

'I propose only one house for all countries, the house of exact breathing' – made in Buenos Aires in 1929, implied the domination of technology over climate. These and other statements laid the foundations for the high-rise corporate office building that dominates the skylines of cities in all continents and has come to be the ubiquitous visible symbol of globalization.

The skyscraper makes use of a standard technological 'kit' of structural frame, curtain-walled envelope, suspended ceiling and air-conditioning to provide an environment for the processes of administration and commerce. Wherever it is located, this 'technical fix' allows the maintenance of similar conditions of temperature, ventilation, humidity and illumination, whether

55

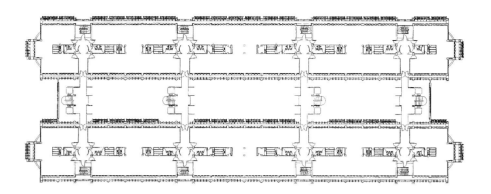

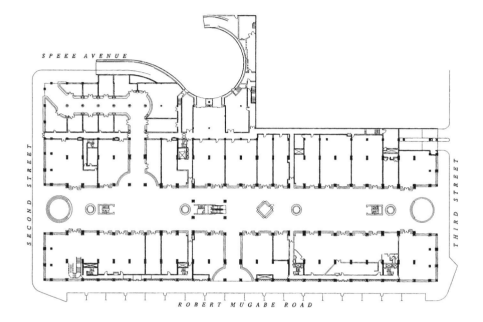

the local climate is hot or cold, dry or humid, temperate, tropical or equatorial.

A 'regional' alternative

The Eastgate Building in Harare offers a powerful challenge to the stereotypical solution. From the beginning the building was designed to provide a good commercial environment without the use of air-conditioning. In the developing economy of Zimbabwe many of the components of environmental plant have to be imported – a process that is expensive and leads to maintenance problems. As an alternative, the designers examined the idea of passive cooling.

The environmental logic of the building makes use of principles widely applied during the 19th century. Eastgate has many

similarities with Barry's and Reid's work at the Palace of Westminster and Jebb's designs for prisons, but there are significant differences, the most obvious of which spring from differences in climate and, to some extent, in function. In addition, computer modelling and, subsequently, quantitative performance modelling invest the design process with a degree of precision that would have been impossible a century and a half ago.

The building occupies an entire city block, 104m by 70m (341ft by 230ft), on the edge of the central business district of Harare. It comprises 26,000m² (279,760ft²) of office space and 5,600m² (60,256ft²) of shops in two, parallel, nine-storey blocks which are oriented with their long axes east–west. Between these is a glass-roofed atrium containing the principal

vertical circulation. The structure is principally reinforced concrete, which plays a crucial role in the environmental strategy. Within the concrete structure the enclosing walls are of brickwork.

The climate of Harare is warm and sunny, with a pattern of warm days and cool nights. Passive cooling works by using this diurnal temperature fluctuation to reduce the temperature of the structure during the night-time hours and, thereby, to reduce the temperature of air delivered to the interior during the day. This is achieved by the complete integration of the building fabric and its environmental processes.

The cross-section illustrates the essentials of the design. The two parallel blocks are 15m (49ft) wide, as is the central atrium. Each block has seven floors of offices above two

←

Plans at ground level, showing the shopping mall, and at a typical upper floor showing the office layout.

Office space under construction, showing the installation of the precast concrete raised floor units. The void between these and the structural concrete slab is the supply plenum for the displacement ventilation system. It also houses electrical services.

↑

General view of office space. The exposed concrete mass of the construction is a fundamental element of the environmental system of the building.

lower floors containing shops, a food court and some parking. Between these zones is a service mezzanine. The incoming air for the offices is drawn through this and is then distributed through a network of vertical ducts. Air is extracted through a second system of ducts and is exhausted through brickwork chimneys above the roof.

The incoming air is taken from the atrium, where it is cleaner than that in the surrounding streets. It is then filtered and driven mechanically through the structure by locally manufactured fans. From the main vertical shafts, air is passed through a void in each concrete floor slab and enters the offices through grilles beneath the windows in the perimeter walls. This low-level supply acts to displace the air in the space, which exits through a high-level vent directly into the vertical extract duct. The extract cycle has no mechanical assistance and is driven entirely by natural stack effect, assisted by the effect of the sun warming the brick chimneys and increasing the velocity of the extracted air. The architect has called these 'solar accelerators'. The building has four principal supply zones that correspond to the four façades – two exposed to the external climate and two to the internal atrium. Cooling is achieved by running the intake fans at a relatively high speed, achieving ten air changes per hour, during the night cycle; this was calculated to provide the best balance between the cooling effect and the amount of power consumed by the fans. During the daytime the fans supply air at only two air changes per hour, which is enough to achieve good ventilation of the offices and to maintain good comfort temperatures. The central atrium is ventilated by stack effect that vents through a gap between the glazed canopy and the roof of the office wings.

For the few occasions when heating is necessary in Harare, the building has individual electric room heaters, located under the windows. These can be controlled by the occupants, but the system is overridden by a thermostatic control to prevent its use when the ambient temperature is above a certain point.

The orientation of Eastgate, with its long façades facing north and south, makes it relatively easy to protect the building from the high angle of the sun at this latitude. All the long elevations, in and outside the atrium, have deep structural overhangs, in the form of precast concrete hoods, and planting to provide shade to the

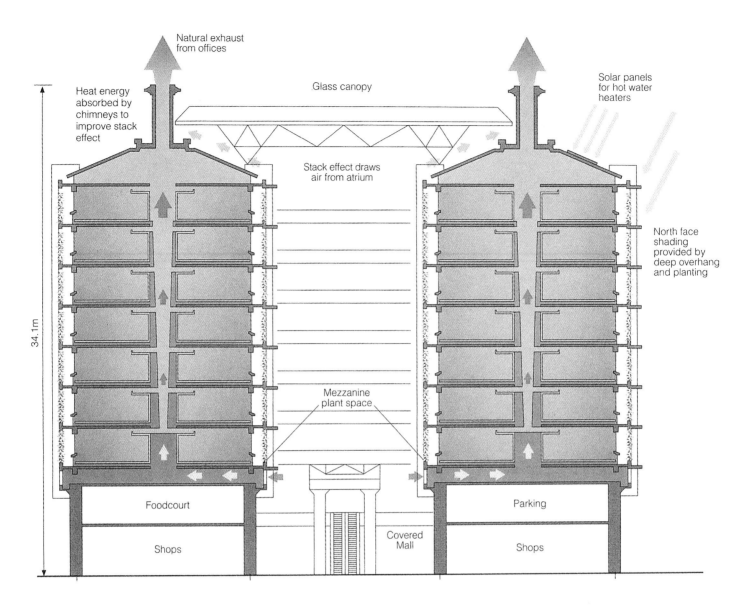

Natural exhaust from offices

Heat energy absorbed by chimneys to improve stack effect

Glass canopy

Solar panels for hot water heaters

Stack effect draws air from atrium

North face shading provided by deep overhang and planting

34.1m

Mezzanine plant space

Foodcourt

Shops

Covered Mall

Parking

Shops

windows. The windows occupy 25 per cent of the façade, and each has an internal blind that can be operated manually to control local solar gains or glare. This ratio was calculated using a computer model which simulated the sun's path and the effect of alternative shading devices, and optimized the balance of lighting and temperature in the offices.

The artificial lighting system is also completely integrated, physically and operationally, into the building. The principal lighting is from fluorescent uplighters suspended from the exposed concrete ceilings, which provide evenly distributed illumination that avoids undesirable reflections on computer screens. The control gear of fluorescent lamps produces heat that would affect the temperature of the offices. To avoid this, they are placed in the exhaust-air

shaft above a lowered ceiling at the rear of the space. This ceiling supports low-energy downlight fittings that supplement the output of the fluorescent lamps.

An array of solar collectors runs along the roof of the northerly block. These are the primary sources for the hot water supplied to the tea kitchens within the offices. They are supplemented by electric heaters, located in the water storage tanks, that can be operated only at night-time.

The performance of the building has been monitored by the consultant engineers, Ove Arup & Partners Zimbabwe, who have established their own offices there. Initial results show that, on days of typical variation in diurnal temperature, 4.5 degrees of cooling of the temperature in the offices can be achieved. When the

diurnal variation is lower, the cooling effect is less marked, but these conditions typically occur when the peak temperature is lower. Initial measurements of total energy consumption indicate that the building performs very well in comparison with recent air-conditioned buildings in Harare. This is in a range of 48 per cent to 83 per cent of the energy demand of these other buildings.

Conclusion
Eastgate stands as a potent symbol of the way in which the standard assumptions and solutions of technological globalism may be challenged by inventive, culturally appropriate and scientifically informed design. The design adapts principles that, as explained in the introduction, have a long and reliable

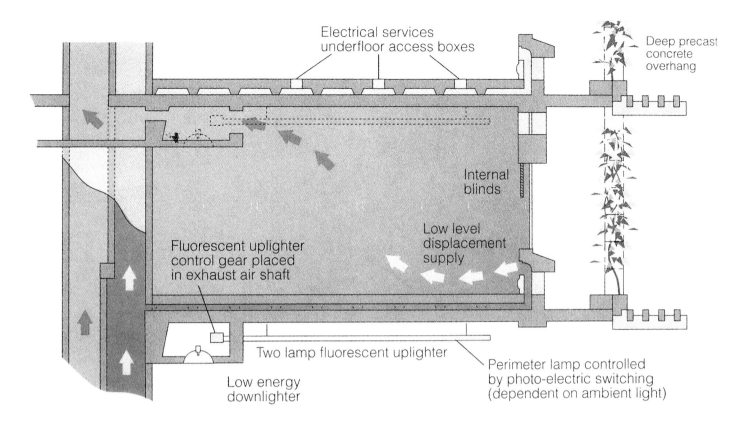

Electrical services
underfloor access boxes

Deep precast
concrete
overhang

Internal
blinds

Fluorescent uplighter
control gear placed
in exhaust air shaft

Low level
displacement
supply

Two lamp fluorescent uplighter

Low energy
downlighter

Perimeter lamp controlled
by photo-electric switching
(dependent on ambient light)

← Operational cross-
section that
describes the
principal features of
the building's
environmental logic.

↑ Detailed cross-
section through a
typical office space.
This shows the
principal air supply
and extract routes
and the integration of

the electrical
installation with the
structure of the
building.

pedigree. With the support of the
analytical and predictive tools that
have emerged from 20th-century
building science, architects and
engineers have collaborated in
investing these principles with a new
precision and reinterpretation. The
result is a building that fits precisely
into its specific economic and
technological and climatological
context.

In achieving this, the building
embodies aspects of the 19th
century's confident synthesis of
structure and environmental process.
It also shows how the 20th century's
engagement with the expression and
organization of the machinery of
environmental control – Louis Kahn's
'served and servant' – can be
reinterpreted in the realization of
passive, selective strategies.

← The central atrium, defined by offices rising above the shopping areas.

→ Detail of the precast concrete shading system that articulates the exterior of the building.

Arup Campus
Arup Associates
Solihull, UK
2001

A question frequently asked by designers who have strongly held practices, philosophies and beliefs is 'Can these tenets survive when the designers become their own developers?' Arup faced this question in the design and construction of their new £7 million Midland headquarters. Although designed by their sister practice, Arup Associates, a brief was set that not only included aspects of effective commercial development, but also focused on the application of the organisation's core skills in comfortable, low-energy and sustainable design. This had to be more than just wishful thinking and

these aspects had to be incorporated into the building in a demonstrable way. The interdisciplinary ethic, for which Arup is famous, also needed to be accommodated spatially.

The brief for the new building specified floor plates that would encourage communication within teams and throughout the company, and provide an appropriate level of flexibility and adaptability. 'We envisaged a new set-up whereby as many diverse Arup skills as possible would be co-located, so that we could co-operate to provide integrated services for the whole range of client requirements. Additionally, we

wanted the offices to be stimulating and efficient, and also represent us to the outside world.' [1]

A vast reservoir of experience is, of course, available. A brief scan of Arup Associates' pedigree in the design of business park-type offices reveals a lineage from the CEGB Headquarters and Wiggins Teape, Basingstoke, through to many phases of Stockley Park, each of which provided lessons that were assimilated into the design of the organization's new building.

Site
The sloping site occupies part of some land earmarked for a proposed

Site plan showing the relationship of the pavilions to the landscape.

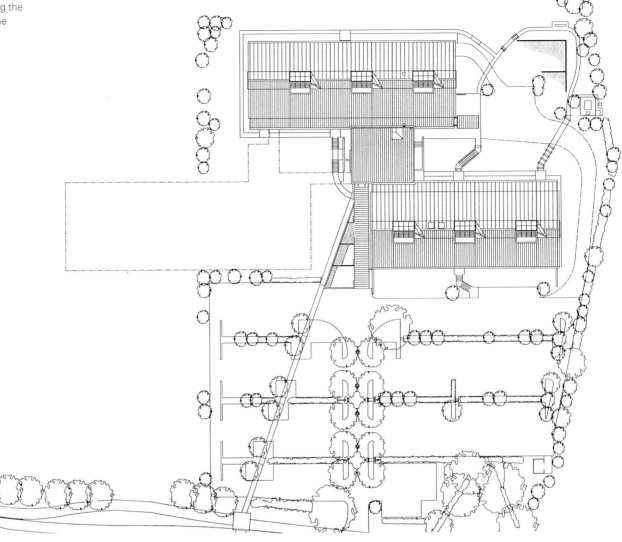

business park in Solihull in the English Midlands. The decision to develop on this particular site was influenced by the need to amalgamate activities previously located in two separate Midlands centres – Birmingham and Coventry.

The positioning of the new buildings is based on the following responses to site:

· exploit panoramic views to the north-west
· exploit and work with the existing site contours
· buildings to address the proposed lake
· accommodate entry from the south, already fixed by the business park distribution road

Furthermore, the development had to be planned for construction in stages. The development will comprise three pavilions (two in Phase 1, and another in Phase 2) that step down the slope of the site. The long dimensions of the pavilions run along the site's contours and take advantage of the views over the lake. At the heart of the plan, an auditorium and café form the focus of the complex. Floors are arranged at half levels and a central link connects the circulation of the Phase 1 pavilions. A central, terraced and landscaped courtyard acts as a potential outdoor work area and social space.

Building Form

The following priorities of the brief have determined the building form:

· a comfortable and energy-efficient working environment
· flexible space

· minimal vertical spatial separation
· a cohesive campus atmosphere
· allowance for tenancy sub-division

The priority for comfort and energy efficiency was further defined as:

· naturally ventilated through outside air supply
· good levels of daylight, contributing to a comfortable visual environment
· a coherent office layout
· visual communication between floors
· views and contacts with outside landscape
· flexibility and adaptability

The formal development of the pavilions is based on these requirements, starting with aspirations for a single space; a clear-span, deep-plan box is described,

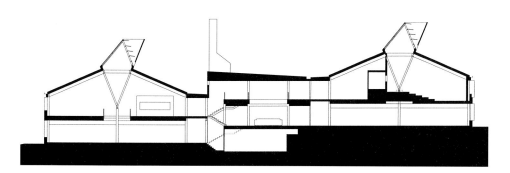

←
Section through
auditorium and office
floor.

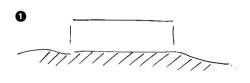

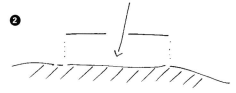

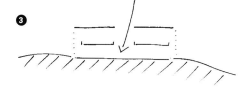

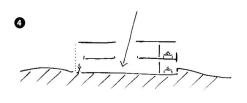

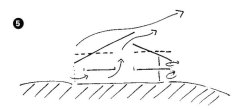

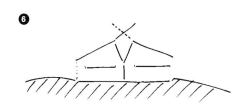

↑

1 A single space...
2 penetrated by light.
3 Cost considerations
   reduce external
   wall: introduction
   of mezzanines...
4 which extend to

   walls to ensure
   lettable space.
5 Pitch roof upward
   to increase internal
   environment then...
6 open structure to
   light with V-supports.

which is then punctured at mid-span roof level to provide daylight. These first two moves are radical, as they break, or at least recast, the mould for the standard campus office model. The desire for daylight and natural ventilation would ordinarily limit the depth of office space to between 12m (39ft) and 14m (46ft). At Solihull, the window-to-window dimension was set at 24m (79ft) almost reverting to the kind of floor plates that would have to rely on a permanently electrically lit and mechanically ventilated interior, like those of the CEGB Headquarters from over 20 years ago. The deep plan deals effectively with the organization's needs; in particular, it can provide the physical context to accommodate a high degree of flexibility and adaptability. Larger spaces, such as auditorium and cafeteria, can fit

alongside a range of different workplace scenarios.

The dumb, and potentially 'exclusive', box is thus transformed into an intelligent, and potentially 'selective', one. The enclosure is layered and pierced to enable daylight penetration and the openings for this, on the ridgeline of a pitched roof, allow for ventilation through stack effect. The environmental section is further developed to optimize daylight and natural modes of ventilation.

Construction and Materials

The buildings are constructed in a sparse, lean and almost stringent manner, sadly not often seen in the UK construction industry. This may have been driven by budget as much as anything else, but it is refreshing to see buildings dealt with in this straightforward way. The structural

system is designed to meet not only the needs of economic structural support, but also the environmental system – embodied energy and re-use. The 24m (79ft) window-to-window dimension is simply split by placing a column at mid-span. This column supports the intermediate floor, then separates into a 'wish-bone' form to hold the two different leaves of the sloping roof apart, to allow daylight penetration. Columns like these, allowing environmental control, are not new to Arup Associates and may be seen as a classic motif, having been employed as early as 1954 in the Duxford Aero Factory.

The steel frame is made visible and exposed, and supports a precast concrete floor and roof panel, which spans 6m (20ft) from beam to beam. The steelwork is bolted to allow

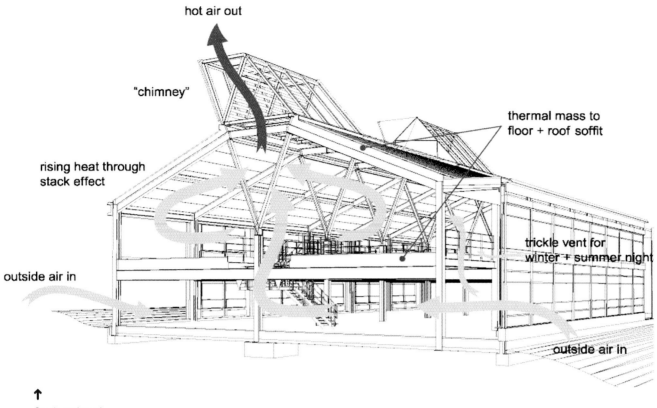

hot air out

"chimney"

thermal mass to
floor + roof soffit

rising heat through
stack effect

trickle vent for
winter + summer night

outside air in

outside air in

↑
Stack-assigned
natural ventilation.

disassembly and re-use at the end of the building's life cycle. The principle of design for re-use runs throughout the building elements, as part of the overall quest for sustainability. Composite construction is eschewed. The soffits of these precast units are left exposed and painted to provide thermal mass.

The external envelope is clad predominantly in untreated western red cedar (from certified, environmentally managed sources) and façades are carefully designed according to orientation. Windows are equipped with moveable, external louvred blinds, again made of cedar, which provide solar control. These windows combine with the opaque façade elements to make refreshingly calm and ordered building façades, which are in stark contrast to the typical call-centre sheds and

speculative office blocks that are its neighbours. The repose of the pavilions is punctuated by aluminium roof 'pods'. These are purpose-designed enclosures that appear at regular intervals and are designed to promote daylight and ventilation. They were designed for ease of assembly and were delivered to site flat-packed, constructed on the ground and erected into position.

Energy and Environment
The design is based on an orthodox approach to the passive design of offices – high levels of daylighting and solar control, with modes of natural ventilation, all within a thermally efficient envelope. The aim of the design team was to achieve a very good rating on the Building Research Establishment Environmental Assessment Method. The building will

probably exceed this standard and achieve an excellent rating, as the combination of passive design (resulting in a reduction in the use of natural resources and CO_2 emissions, and greater recycling) and global factors, such as transport (a Green Transport Plan has been devised for occupiers) add up to an integrated approach to the Campus.

Visual environment
The areas and disposition of glazing were determined in the physical and computer modelling carried out by Arup Associates and in the Artificial Sky at the Bartlett faculty, University College London. In particular, studies were made to ensure that the glare index from perimeter windows and roof-mounted pods was controlled. Daylighting is achieved through the combination of top and sidelight by

↑ Design sketch section shows pavilions sited on contours.

→ Early design sketches illustrate environmental principles and formal development.

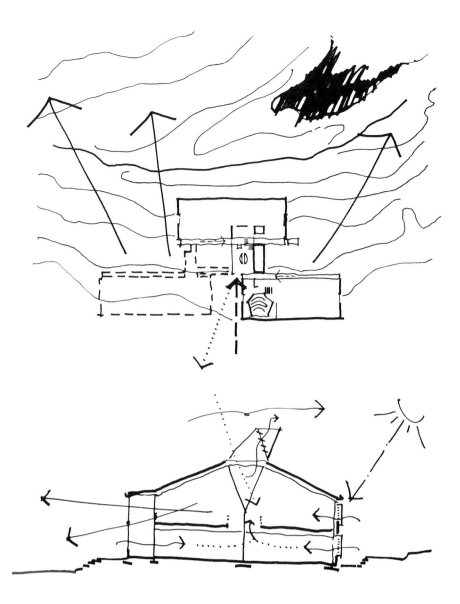

external louvres and manually operated shutters to south façades, and manually and electrically operated internal blinds to other façades.

The lighting systems have been designed to achieve a 400 lux level of illumination over the work surface. Whilst much of this is through daylight during normal working hours, an automatic lighting control system is linked to, and balances, lighting conditions.

Ventilation

The office is designed for natural ventilation under most conditions. Defying the current orthodoxy of 14m (46ft) floor plates, window to window, the Campus floor plate is a ground-breaking 24m (79ft). The ridgeline 'pods' supplement normal passive design strategies. The perimeter walls incorporate windows with openable vents at high and low levels. Trickle vents, linked to the building management system, add to these openings. In summer conditions, windows are opened as necessary, this being linked to stack effect ventilation via the roof pods. Draught-free, controlled ventilation is achieved in the winter by motorized louvres, designed as integral parts of the cladding system. The same mechanisms operate to provide useful night-time cooling.

Heating is provided by a simple low-pressure hot-water system, with perimeter radiators, again linked to the building management system. A number of temperature sensors are located throughout the building and activate the building management system, which operates the damper devices to control ventilation rates.

The auditorium and computer rooms are air-conditioned, based on a displacement system, with free cooling using outside air for the majority of the year.

Conclusion

For many designers, it seems obvious that sustainability should be integral to the development of architectural practice. However, more often than not, atypical projects tend to get this kind of treatment – landmark projects or, at the other end of the scale, modest projects designed by environmentally committed practitioners. Sustainability is worn on the sleeve of the completed buildings. To attempt to transform the established and well-known typeform, in order to achieve high performance, may be a tougher challenge than making bespoke buildings and, in the

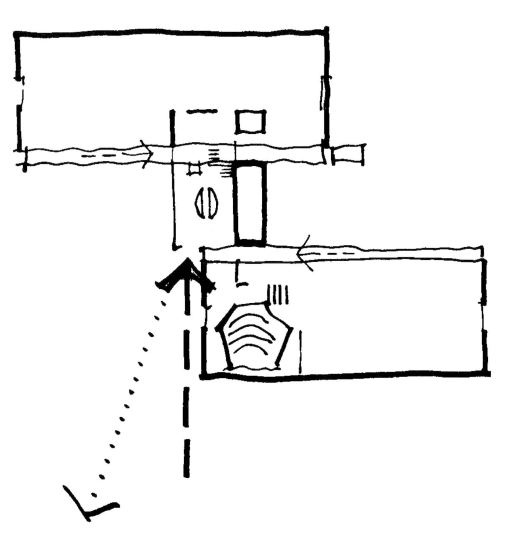

←
Design sketch
showing the entrance
sequence.

↓
Sectional model.

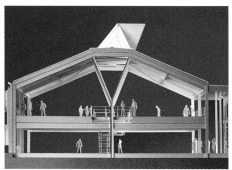

long run, may be more important. At
Solihull, a new approach to the design
of the office campus building has
been adopted and the resulting
architecture is relaxed, site-
responsive and stringent, but also
humanely modern. It also has green
credentials. Taking on such challenges
places particular demands on the
design team who set and pursue
these goals. Mindsets have to be
changed, research and validation
takes place in the midst of fast-track
development and the results,
although significant, rarely make the
pages of the respected architectural
journals.

←
Campus under
construction: the
wishbone atrium at
mid-span.

↑
Solar control to the
campus pavilion
façades.

First-floor offices:
daylit interior.

→
The dynamic façade
provides
environmental
control for the user.

↓
Detail of window.

→
Roof-mounted 'pod'
structures for
daylight and natural
ventilation.

Howlands Farm Student Housing
Arup Associates
Durham, UK
1999

→
General view showing
brick pavilions and
timber ventilation
towers.

Nikolaus Pevsner described Durham as 'one of the great experiences of Europe....The group of cathedral, castle and monastery on the rock can only be compared to Avignon and Prague.'[1] The University of Durham was founded in 1832 and received its first students the following year. University College took over the castle, which had been the seat of the prince-bishops of Durham, and during the first century of the university's existence its principal institutions and buildings were accommodated on the rock, woven into the tissue of the old city. In response to the expansion of British universities that began in the 1960s, new buildings, including teaching departments and student housing, were built in open country to the south of the city.

The expansion continued, and in 1994 the university held an architectural competition, won by Arup Associates, for the design of more student housing on a site at Howlands Farm on the crest of a south-west-facing slope. The competition brief was for an extensive development, which Arup Associates conceived as a hilltop 'village' of 21 individual 'villas' and a large communal building. The programme for the project explicitly asked for an environmentally responsible approach. Requirements ranged in scale from a request that all excavated construction material should be kept on the site to a prescription that the

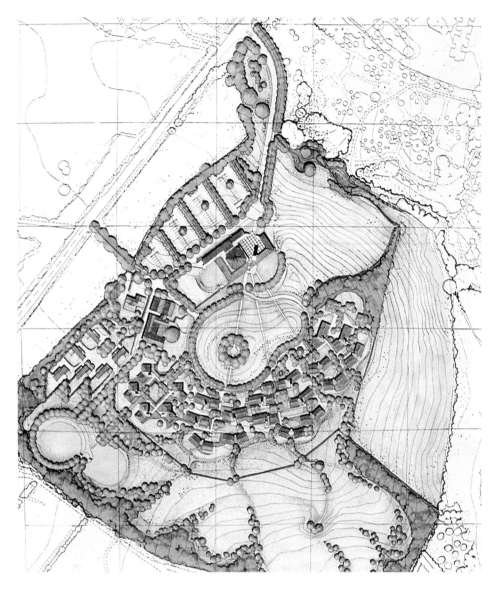

↑
Interior of study-bedroom.

←
Site plan.

individual buildings should achieve low overall energy consumption. The first stage of the project, consisting of eight villas and a small communal building converted from an existing barn, has been completed.

Dwelling form and energy use
Early in the 1970s, immediately after the energy crisis, much of the pioneering research into low-energy design focused on using small houses to test the principles of harnessing solar power – a process that continues to the present day. In many respects, this approach underlies Arup Associates' design at Howlands Farm, which opens up the possibility of a domestic-scale solution to a project that, in other interpretations, could have been larger and more monolithic.

There are, of course, significant differences between the design of a single-family house and a collective dwelling for a community of students. Student accommodation requires a different spatial organization from that of a house. In the Durham development, the plan form of each three-storey villa consists of two blocks containing simple study-bedroom cells. A linking element contains the entrance and the staircase, and the configuration of this in relation to the accommodation blocks is adjusted in response to the building's location and its relation to its neighbours.

Within this general form there are three variations in the accommodation provided. Five of the villas each provide accommodation for 21 students, including one shower room shared between two and a kitchen shared between seven. Two other buildings have a more complex mix, with 29 study-bedrooms, each with its own washbasin, but with the shower rooms each shared between three students, and the kitchens each shared between four or six students. The final block of the nine so far completed has en suite bathrooms for each of its 28 study-bedrooms, and the kitchens are shared between either nine or ten students.

In a single-family house the daytime rooms – the living room, dining room and kitchen – usually account for at least 50 per cent of the total floor area. In most passive solar designs the aim is to maximize the potential solar gains to reduce the requirement for conventional space heating. It is the daytime spaces that benefit most from this, and one of the fundamental principles of passive design applied to house design is to provide the principal rooms with a southerly

Internal courtyard
dominated by
ventilation tower.

Site model.

orientation to maximize the capture of solar heat.

At Howlands Farm the predominance of individual study-bedrooms over communal spaces has led to a different interpretation. In their load-bearing brick construction, with small window openings and strongly expressed concrete lintels and sills, the simple forms of the residential blocks allude to the 19th-century industrial vernacular housing of the former coal-mining villages that surround the city of Durham. As with those dwellings, there is no preferential orientation of the individual rooms. A significant difference is that the new buildings are constructed to a very high standard of thermal insulation. With their relative compactness of form, the new buildings suffer a low overall heat loss, thereby reducing energy demand.

It is at the junction of the two blocks that the passive design strategy is brought to bear. The entrance and staircase block becomes both a solar collector and the motive power for a system of natural ventilation that serves all the shower rooms, lavatories, kitchens and communal spaces. The external expression of these facilities is found in the large south-facing windows that enclose the stairwells and, most dramatically, in the brick ventilation shafts, surmounted by tall timber 'wind-catchers', which rise above the entrances.

Passive energy systems

The wind towers are used as inlets and outlets for the natural ventilation system. Each tower is divided vertically to form two stacks. One captures incoming air and delivers this downwards through a duct

network to the spaces below. A parallel network of ducts carries the extracted air back to the tower and away through the other stack. The extract stack is equipped with a heat exchanger that, in winter, removes heat from the warm exhaust air and transfers it to the adjacent stack to preheat the incoming fresh air. A fan has been installed to guarantee that the building is adequately ventilated on the few days when the air is still.

In passive design terminology, the glazed stairwells operate as a 'direct gain' system. In this, the direct insolation raises the temperature of the air, which is circulated by the ventilation system into the communal spaces. Absorbed heat continues to be re-radiated from the heavy masonry construction of the stairwells and partitions at night, after the sun has set and the temperature begins to

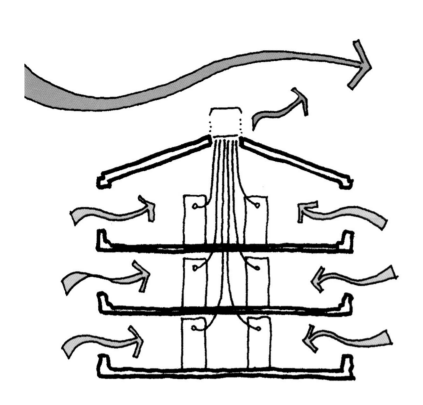

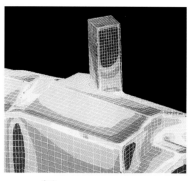

Pressure
Relative PA
Local:
max 0.6320
min 0.9471

CFD model output
showing pressure
distribution over the
building envelope.

Cross-section
showing ventilation
processes.

View from the south
showing ventilation
tower and glazed
staircase block.

fall, helping to spread the useful heat through the diurnal cycle.

Conclusion

The Durham project is, at first sight, modest in its ambitions and unremarkable in its architectural language. But, as is often the case, appearances are deceptive. There is a deep strand of British architecture, characterized by J. M. Richards as 'the Functional Tradition', that rests on the celebration of the necessary, and it is in this lineage that Howlands Farm takes its place.[2] Its originality comes not from contrived novelty but from the transformation of the conventional. The simple, strong brick volumes and pitched roofs of the villas conceal new standards of construction and performance. It is the juxtaposition of these forms with the glazed expanses of the stairwells and the vertical extension of the ventilation towers that produces something new. Everything is expressive of its purpose.

The apparent simplicity of this project may seem out of place in the wider discourse about the relationship between architect and engineer, but such apparently effortless integration of form and performance requires mutual understanding and unity of purpose within the design team equal to that necessary to produce the more demonstrable synthesis evident in large-scale, technologically complex designs.

Marzahn Low-Energy Apartment Building, Assmann, Salomon & Scheidt Berlin, Germany 1994–97

➜
View from south-east
showing glazed
façade.

One of the key questions in the design of a building is the selection of its fundamental form. The history of architecture shows how certain forms have been consistently used, adapted or transformed to meet recurrent and changing needs. In *The Classical Language of Architecture*, Summerson shows how building forms that were first established in antiquity have proved to be appropriate models for many subsequent buildings.[1] For example, the cylindrical form of the Pantheon in Rome, with its attached portico, has been adapted to serve as, among many uses, church, dwelling,

academic institution and public library. Reference to past forms was given more formal recognition and structure at the beginning of the 19th century through the development of the idea of type by theoreticians such as J. N. L. Durand.[2]

Our contemporary concern about the design of low-energy buildings means that the question of form, and its relation to typology, has a new and important role to play. 'What shape is a low-energy building?' is an obvious and easy question to ask, but the answer is neither obvious nor necessarily easy. One assumption made in some of the early theoretical

studies of the question was that there is a direct relation between the ratio of the surface area of a form and the volume it encloses; because energy is consumed in compensating for heat loss, it seemed self-evident that an efficient form would be that which minimized the surface area to volume ratio. A quarter of a century ago the literature was scattered with confident statements such as: 'Buildings should be large rather than small and have circular or square plans, heated buildings should be near cubical in shape.'[3] Subsequently, these simple prescriptions were more thoroughly investigated, and the complexity of

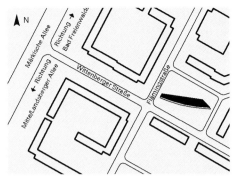

←
Site plan.

←
Typology of 'primitive' built forms.

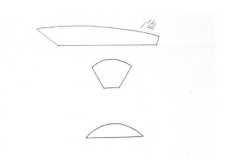

↑
View from south-east showing projecting balconies that provide shade in the summer months.

→
The minimally glazed north façade.

the question is now more thoroughly understood, but the question of shape remains at the heart of low-energy design – and it is this that makes the design of the apartment building at Marzahn in Berlin of such great interest.[4]

The development of form

Marzahn is a suburb of eastern Berlin where the client, a housing association, sought to build 56 apartments. The housing association had entered into an agreement with the local government by which they would qualify for additional funding as long as the design achieved a target for energy demand 20 per cent below the newly introduced regulations. The client determined that the design should, from the outset, be subject to a close collaboration between the architects and the consultant engineers. In addition to their conventional responsibilities for structure and building services, Arup had been appointed as energy consultant.

The design process began with a study of the relationship between form and energy use. During the cold Berlin winters the principal demand for energy would be in space heating, so the researchers looked at the question of surface area to volume. A typology of six 'primitive' built forms was constructed. In plan these were a square, a rectangle, a circle, a semicircle, an arc and a truncated fan-shape. All were assumed to be six storeys high and with a gross floor area of 6,000m² (64,560ft²). Calculations were made to assess the annual heating energy demand for each of the forms to enable comparisons to be made. In making the calculations, standard assumptions were made about the insulation value of the envelope and, crucially, allowance was made for the contribution to heating requirement that would be made by solar heat gain from the southerly orientation. In the extended forms it was assumed that the long façade would face south, a condition that could be met on the site for the building.

The results of the study showed that a cylindrical building would, at 35kWh/m² (11.09 BthU/ft²), have the lowest winter-heat energy demand of the first five built forms. But the truncated fan shape could, by a process of manipulation of its proportions, be shown to equal this. To achieve this result, the north façade was kept as short as possible and the lengths of the east and west façades were varied systematically until an

'optimum' was reached. The advantage of this form, in comparison with the cylinder, is that all the apartments could have a southerly aspect.

The determination of the overall built form is only the starting point in the design of any building. The initial studies were followed by more detailed investigations into the arrangement and detailed design of the individual apartments within the block. These led to a particular plan form in which the principal rooms – living room, kitchen and bedrooms – face south, and the entrances, hallways and bathrooms are all located at the north side. Beyond these the circulation areas, containing lifts and stairs, act as an unheated buffer zone. The curved façade means that the precise orientation of the individual apartments varies, so they

do not enjoy equal amounts of solar gain throughout the day. To allow the inhabitants to overcome this to some degree, the partitions between these rooms have sliding doors that allow the entire apartment to be opened up to the sun.

The building is constructed with load-bearing cross-walls of precast concrete that form the divisions between the apartments. The floors are also precast units, prestressed to span 8.6m (28ft). The internal partitions within the apartments are non-loadbearing. The envelope is constructed to a high standard of thermal insulation, typically less than $0.2W/m^2/°C$ (0.035 BthU/ft^2/°C), and the glazing is specified to balance heat loss and the collection of useful solar gain.

Structure and service
In the general terminology of environmental architecture, the design that evolved through this analytical process is described as 'direct-gain, passive-solar'. In some instances, and in certain climates, it may be possible to design a building using the principles of passive-solar design that achieves acceptable levels of thermal comfort without recourse to any auxiliary heating system. In Berlin's relatively extreme winter climate, and in the design of mass-housing, it would be difficult to contemplate such a solution. But the integration of an auxiliary heating system with passive solar elements is not a trivial task. The heating system uses hot water supplied, via a heat exchanger, from a local district heating network. The rooms are heated by conventional radiators.

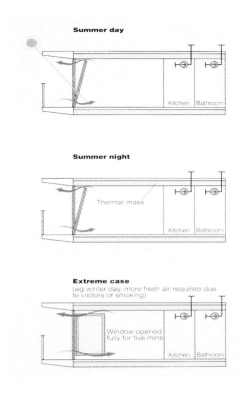

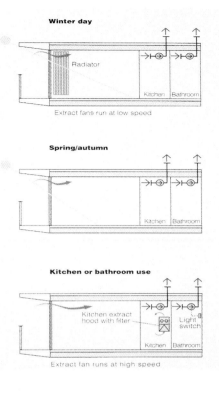

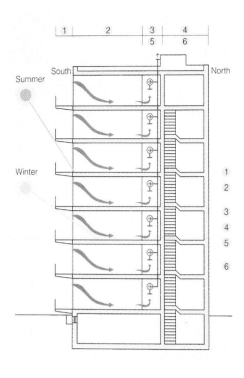

Detailed cross-sections showing seasonal and diurnal operation of the environmental systems.

↑
Cross-section showing assisted ventilation of appartments.

In a highly insulated building there is a risk that heat loss due to uncontrolled ventilation could be extremely wasteful. To avoid this, each apartment at Marzahn has two extract fans, one in the kitchen, the other in the bathroom. These provide most of the ventilation that is needed in winter by drawing fresh air in through controllable vents in the window frames of the south-facing rooms. If there is a need for more ventilation, the large windows can be opened, but when this is done the heating system and the mechanical ventilation are automatically turned off. This quickly lowers the room temperature and implicitly instructs the inhabitants about how to get the best out of their building.

The building has a computer-controlled building management system that, in addition to linking the heating system to the opening windows, allows the users to receive, from a touch screen display in each apartment, information about their energy consumption (expressed in Deutschmarks), room temperatures and so forth. The hope is that these data will further inform the inhabitants about the performance of the building and, thereby, produce greater efficiency of use.

In the summer months the building is naturally ventilated and the overhang of the continuous balconies of the south façade provides solar shading. The depth of the overhang was calculated to balance winter insolation with summer shading, and further shading, if required, is provided by internal blinds. A group of deciduous trees provides more shade but allows the sun to reach the building in winter when they have shed their leaves. The building management system provides a visible warning to the occupant at times when the windows could provide more effective ventilation than the mechanical fans. It is intended that the windows should be left open on summer nights, both to provide ventilation and to cool the thermal mass of the exposed ceilings. This will then assist in maintaining comfort temperatures during the following day.

Conclusion
In architecture the relationship between theory and practice is complex. The design office and the building site frequently play as important a part in the development of theory as the research institute. The lesson of Marzahn is a clear example of this. The design of an apparently

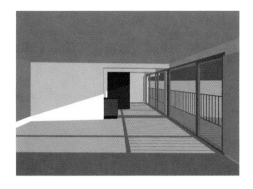  

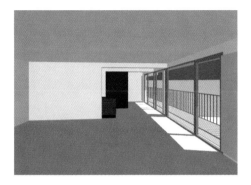 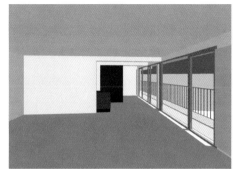 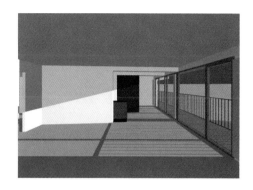

 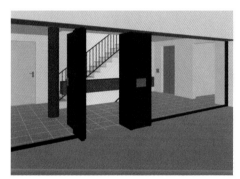

←
Computer simulation
of sunlight
penetration into
appartments and
circulation space.

straightforward building project proves to be a valuable vehicle for research into the relationship between built form and performance. The studies carried out here by the design team show how simple prescriptions may be refined to add to the evolving typology of low-energy architecture. The further development of the design, through its constructional system, detailed planning and its mechanical services and their controls, shows that the technical success of a building depends equally upon its practical realization as upon its initial conception.

To return to broader questions of form, type and architectural method, it is interesting to compare the Marzahn design, the product of an explicitly systematic design procedure, with Alvar Aalto's 'Neue Vahr' apartment building in Bremen, designed in 1958

and completed in 1962.[5] At that date, low-energy design was not acknowledged as part of the main agenda of architecture, but the work of many architects evinced a profound, often intuitive, sense of the interdependence of architecture and nature, and between architecture and environment. Among the major architects of the 20th century, Aalto exhibited this sensibility more than most: 'a truly serious problem is the discovery of form, the basic design for our century'.

The Bremen building logically and eloquently responds to the environmental difference of north and south exposures, closed and orthogonal to the north, open and undulating to the south. It is certain that Marzahn will be superior to Neue Vahr in its energy performance – the explicit energy brief will guarantee

that. On the other hand, the similarity between it and the product of Aalto's informed intuition about architecture's place in relation to nature serves to connect the new building, and the research that it embodies, to the significant mainstream. The development of architecture as a comprehensive discipline, embracing the arts and the sciences, will only be properly achieved if we make connections, as Le Corbusier urged in *Vers une architecture*, between the realms of objectivity and intuition.[6]

← Appartment interior showing sliding partitions between the principal rooms.

↑ South façade.

→
Staircase hall.

↓
Detail of south-facing glazing.

BedZED Sustainable Development

Bill Dunster
London, UK
2002

➜
BEDZED is a
compact live/work
development that
exploits the potential
for sustainable
futures.

In 1999 the UK government published *Towards an Urban Renaissance*, a report that aimed to provide guidelines for practical solutions to the design of cities, towns and urban neighbourhoods. It claimed to establish 'a new vision for urban regeneration founded on the principles of design excellence, social well being and environmental responsibility within a viable economic and legislative framework'. [1]

Counter-urbanization was one of several factors identified to have contributed directly to 20 per cent increases in energy consumption by households in England over the previous 25 years. Underperformance in waste management and increases in motor-vehicle traffic were also contributors to the huge environmental burden. The report's conclusions were that a much greater

mix of building types and tenures in more compact urban forms close to existing and new transport interchanges were needed.

The London borough of Sutton took up the challenge in the form of the Beddington Zero Energy Development, a ground-breaking project that aims to prove that sustainable living is not only economically and technically viable

↑
The development includes a number of community facilities.

↑
The BedZED layout consists of five rows of terraces, running east–west.

but can also be comfortable and manageable for ordinary people. The development has its roots in a collaboration between Bioregional Developments, an environmental charity, and Bill Dunster Architects. BedZED is designed to provide 82 homes and 1,600m² (17,220ft²) of work space on a 1.4ha (3½ acre) site, as well as a number of other facilities, including a sports club, a football pitch, a nursery, an organic-food shop and a health centre. BedZED is the largest sustainable development of its kind in the UK, and it anticipated in many ways the outcome of recent UK planning policies.

The BedZED strategy for sustainable design is holistic, embracing health and safety, water-use efficiency, recycling, waste minimization and green transport as well-known principles of low-energy design.

Heating requirements in a BedZED home are expected to be around 10 per cent of those of a typical UK home of the same size.

Site, location and climate

The site, a former sewage works on the southern edge of London, was sold to the client, Peabody Trust, even though BedZED was not the highest bidder. For the first time in the UK, a scheme's sustainability credentials had been taken into account in the adjudication of tenders. Peabody, however, was not sole developer of the site. The site was found by environmental advisers Bioregional Developments, who approached Peabody for funding. The core of Bioregional's design team had been developing the design to a relatively detailed stage prior to Peabody's involvement. The site is 15 minutes'

walk from Mitcham station and on the new Wimbledon to Croydon tramline. Anticipating many of the principles discussed in *Towards an Urban Renaissance* by architect Lord Richard Rogers, head of Britain's Urban Task Force, the designers addressed the question of how to build an urban community that provides a high-quality lifestyle without profligate use of scarce global resources.

The layout is very straightforward: five rows of terraces run east–west. This results in an overall density of 50 dwellings and 120 workspaces per hectare after allowing for the sports facility, clubhouse and landscaping. The design team estimates that approximately 1½ million dwellings of this kind could be built on existing 'brownfield' land in the UK – satisfying almost half the predicted need by 2016.

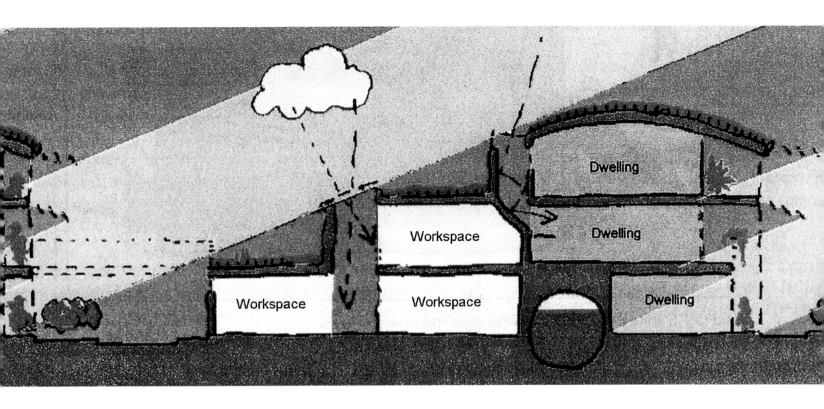

↑
Sketch section
depicting solar
strategy.

Houses are placed on the south side of the terraces to promote maximum solar potential and workspaces are on the north side, shaded by the dwellings, and may therefore be north-lit and naturally ventilated. Although the layout is compact, green amenity space is made available wherever possible – for example, workspace roofs are used as gardens for adjacent dwellings. In this way, every dwelling has a private garden at densities that would normally only allow for balconies. This relieves the scheme of the monotonous one-dimensional layouts of the early generation of passive solar housing schemes. The integrated nature of the project with its social amenities and shared community spaces is more closely related, in fact, to the garden suburb model.

Construction and materials
The thermal performance of the building envelope at BedZED is three times more efficient than the current UK regulations require and will also outstrip projected performance standards for 2003; 300mm (12in) thickness of insulation provides U values that still justify description of 'super-insulated dwelling'. The building form is clearly based on Hope House, Bill Dunster's own house built four years earlier.[2] Although built as a 'one-off', the house has always been considered a prototype for a high-density form of urban dwelling. The original house can be defined as a classic solar design, with a south-facing conservatory backed up by a well-insulated fabric with high thermal mass. As at Hope House, thermal mass – provided by intermediate concrete floors – is an

integral part of the strategy of the BedZED dwellings.

BedZED is built from natural recycled materials. New wood is sourced from FSC (Forest Stewardship Council) sources and all other materials have been sourced within a 35 mile (56km) radius of the site, often using salvaged materials especially for timber studwork. Energy and pollution generated from transport is thereby kept to a minimum and the local economy benefits. Local contractors are preferred. The BedZED philosophy of employing local resources to deal with global concerns is one of the first examples of 'glocal' architecture in the UK.

Building form
The typical modern dwelling in the UK has a relatively low occupancy, low intermittent heat gains and a wide

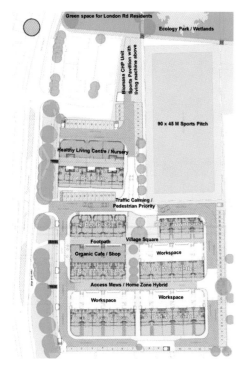

Green space for London Rd Residents
Ecology Park / Wetlands
Biomass CHP Unit
Sports Pavilion with living machine above
90 x 45 M Sports Pitch
Healthy Living Centre / Nursery
Traffic Calming / Pedestrian Priority
Footpath
Village Square
Organic Cafe / Shop
Workspace
Access Mews / Home Zone Hybrid
Workspace
Workspace

↑
Site layout.

BedZED U VALUES OUTSTRIP PROJECTED UK STANDARDS				
Element	Fabric U values W/m²/°K (Btu/h/ft²/°F) Current value	Proposed value for 2001	Proposed value for 2003	Bedzed value
roof	0.25 (0.044)	0.2 (0.035)	0.16 (0.028)	0.1 (0.018)
ground floor	0.45 (0.079)	0.3 (0.053)	0.25 (0.044)	0.1 (0.018)
exposed floor	0.45 (0.079)	0.3 (0.053)	0.25 (0.044)	0.1 (0.018)
exposed walls	0.45 (0.079)	0.35 (0.062)	0.3 (0.053)	0.11 (0.019)
windows, doors and rooflights	3.3 (0.581)	2.2 (0.387)	2 (0.352)	1.2 (0.211)

↑
Table showing how U values at BedZED exceed projected UK standards.

→
Ventilation strategy for both dwelling and work spaces.

range of summer comfort conditions. There are huge potential benefits in energy and comfort terms from south-facing passive solar heating. On the other hand, the workplace has high internal heat gains and a more precisely defined comfort range. The consequence is often installation of expensive solar-shading devices, high lighting use and uneven daylighting provision across the workspace. These features combined to provide the design team with straightforward solutions in terms of building form:

· dwellings are orientated south in terraces
· workspaces are orientated north in terraces
· terraces are positioned to avoid overshadowing, wherever possible
· heat loss through exposed surface area is minimized

· south-facing glazed sun spaces are included in all dwellings.

Design for sustainability
Sustainable design aims not only to reduce our dependence on non-renewable resources but also addresses issues of environmental impact, social progress and economic prosperity. The design team at BedZED have taken a step towards a holistic approach to the design of new housing schemes, aiming to make sustainable living 'easy, attractive and affordable'. They have put the following issues at the forefront of the project:

· reduction in energy demand and renewable sourcing
· land reuse, higher than normal urban density and biodiversity through landscape design

· integration with existing communities
· innovative home/work arrangements
· reduced travel for material miles, food miles, home/work miles
· promotion of walking, cycling and use of public transport
· material environmental impact, embodied energy, durability and recycling
· reduced water consumption
· consumable waste and recycling
· buildings as energy producers for transport.

Energy demand
The objective is to match energy demand with available renewable energy sources so that the buildings at BedZED do not add to carbon dioxide emissions in the atmosphere. Renewable energy sources in the UK

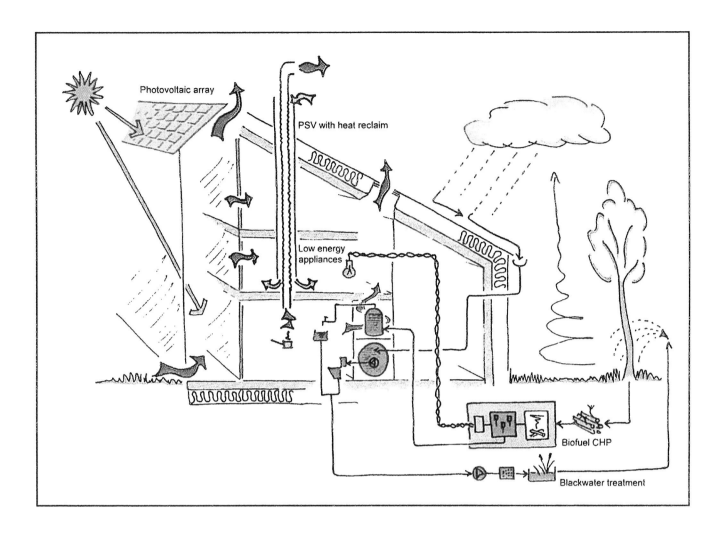

Photovoltaic array

PSV with heat reclaim

Low energy appliances

Biofuel CHP

Blackwater treatment

are difficult to match and balance with demand as well as being expensive in terms of capital costs. It is therefore vital to reduce energy demand through other design strategies, for example, high-performance building fabric.

As BedZED consists of a mixture of dwellings, office shops and community accommodation, Arup initially carried out a review of typical energy consumption for the various building types and established target consumption figures. The grade of energy being consumed was also considered. In the UK, in general terms, electricity is the highest-grade energy and is the most difficult to replace through renewable sources. The production of hot water is the next most difficult, and space heating is the easiest. As a result of this early analysis the following design principles were adopted:

· super-insulation to match fabric heat loss to internal and passive solar gain
· room surface has high thermal capacity to store internal heat until needed
· passive cooling using thermal mass to avoid mechanical cooling
· reduction of uncontrolled ventilation and air infiltration
· avoidance of parasitic energy by mechanical means (high grade energy...by fans, pumps, etc.)
· installing systems that are easy to understand and operate manually
· ventilation heat recovery
· good natural daylight
· high-efficiency initiatives
· low-energy domestic appliances

Energy sources
The following renewable sources of energy were identified by the design team as useful for BedZED:

· passive solar heating
· heat from occupants
· heat from lighting and appliances
· heat from cooking and domestic hot water
· daylight
· bio-fuelled combined heat and power unit (CHP)

It was proposed that BedZED would become a nett producer of energy through the use of renewable resources. The building of integrated photovoltaics was also proposed to provide power for electric cars. Low-grade energy for space heating will be provided by passive solar means combined with internal heat gains. For the system to operate successfully, an efficient means of storing low-grade heat is essential. At BedZED extensive exposed high-thermal-capacity room surfaces will absorb heat when room

BIO-FUELLED COMBINED HEAT & POWER
CHP

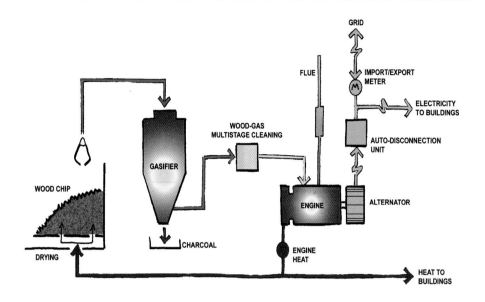

Bio-fuel system for the development.

temperatures start to rise and release heat back into the atmosphere when temperatures fall.

A combined heat and power unit (CHP) fuelled by chipped and dried tree waste will generate BedZED's electricity. The nominal 130KW capacity CHP is equipped with an export/import connection to the national grid, allowing constant electrical output of the CHP to balance demand changes. By eliminating space-heating loads which fluctuate through seasonal demand, a more constant heat output can be designed for the CHP. For example, the CHP supplies domestic hot water whose daily total demand is relatively constant all year round. Some heat storage is needed to deal with daily fluctuations, however, and this is provided by large domestic hot-water cylinders in each dwelling and

workplace. The CHP 'trickle' charges them and the peak hot-water demand is designed to match the peak CHP output, thereby avoiding the cost of peak-load boiler plant. Cylinder immersion heaters provide a hot-water standby. Energy meters are located in prominent positions so that users can monitor their own energy consumption.

Daylighting
A primary goal of the BedZED team is to provide good daylighting in offices and dwellings in order to save energy through reduced use of electric light and also to improve the overall visual environment. Daylighting in offices is considered especially important because offices are used predominantly during the day and have higher illumination requirements. Particular attention was paid to the

sectional development of the terraces and window design. The performance characteristics of the windows in dwellings were defined as follows:

· low emissivity
· clear triple-glazing to all windows
· clear double glazing on room side and exterior of solar spaces
· daylight obstruction through frame to be no greater than 30 per cent
· windows to have larger panes due to both internal and external framing obstruction
· average room surface to be reflective

Ventilation
The strategy at BedZED is 'build tight and ventilate right' to limit ventilation heat loss and eliminate the need for a conventional heating system. It is based on using natural ventilation to minimize capital costs and energy

consumption. Ventilation is needed for fresh air, periodic purging (of pollutants), cooling during occupancy, night-time cooling, removal of local moisture gains and removal of smells.

The BedZED design is founded on the provision of occupant-controlled opening windows of an area equal to at least 5 per cent of the floor area in all habitable rooms. For night-time cooling, secure locking allows windows to be held with a minimum clear 50mm (2in) opening. Wind- and winter buoyancy-driven roof cowls supply fresh air and extract moisture and pollutants.

In naturally ventilated domestic and non-domestic buildings a minimum supply of fresh air is normally provided by window trickle ventilators. However, in a low-energy building without room-heat emitters, such ventilators become a significant

energy drain, particularly on a cold windy day. Ventilation design for BedZED seeks to provide preheated fresh air by using passive stack ventilation with heat recovery. This takes advantage of the sealed building envelope to create a balanced air supply and exhaust using a combination of internal heat buoyancy and wind pressure through a both positive and negative heat exchanger fitted with a roof wind cowl. The air supply enters the living rooms and bedrooms, and the exhaust comes from the kitchens, bathrooms and toilets.

Mechanical systems

The low-energy strategy is based on exploiting the use of low-tech building fabric form and materials and avoiding heavy dependence on sophisticated electrical and

mechanical systems in the individual buildings. Large capital investments have been made in providing the long-life passive building fabric components, while savings have been made by not supplying conventional heating systems. Over the long design life of the building this strategy will result in the lowest 'cradle-to-grave', embodied and consumed energy needs. The mechanical services systems consist of:

· potable water supply from mains
· rainwater greywater system
· domestic hot water cylinder assembly in each dwelling/workspace
· site-wide bio-fuelled mini-CHP serving each domestic hot-water cylinder
· wind and passive stack drum ventilation with heat recovery

Heating

The strategy is to avoid the need for a conventional mechanical system by designing the building fabric so that the natural heat gains are more than adequate to cope with the heat losses. This is achieved by using:

· heat gains from people
· heat gains from lighting and appliances
· heat gains from cooking and domestic hot water
· solar heat gain
· super-insulation
· very high envelope air-tightness
· ventilation heat recovery
· high thermal inertia room surfaces to store excess heat until it is needed

The goal is to achieve room temperatures almost constantly above 19°C (66°F) if occupants wish. Alternatively, rooms can be vented by opening windows manually. During longer periods when the building is unoccupied, and therefore experiencing minimum heat gains, the aim is to maintain a background temperature using a thermostatically controlled vent from the domestic hot-water cylinder cupboard. The piped CHP primary hot-water mains serve the domestic hot-water needs of the buildings through a coil inside the hot-water cylinders of each dwelling and workspace. The CHP main return pipe goes via a bathroom towel rail in each dwelling.

Water consumption

One of the aims of the project is to reduce potable water consumption by avoiding power showers and installing outlet-flow limiters and low-water-consuming appliances. A range of water-recycling methods has been investigated, with the recovery of rainwater to serve low-water flush toilets being identified as most suitable. Design aims are as follows:

· potable water demand could be reduced by about 50 per cent
· water system has low mechanical plant requirement
· proven component availability
· self-cleaning filtration
· almost no maintenance
· standard drainage components, eg. rainwater store is a large drainage pipe
· main roof as impermeable collection surface, as it should be noted that garden and street run-off unsuitable due to fouling by animals, cars and garden chemicals

←
Community building
flanking the
recreation area.

↑
The integrated
sustainable
community.

Conclusion

BedZED is the most ambitious
sustainable development in the UK.
Designed to be energy-efficient, it is
based on well-known and orthodox
technologies, but it goes way beyond
the previous generations of 'low-
energy' housing. It is based on a new
way of integrated communal living.
This is not as new or radical in other
mainland European countries as it is
in England, where the general quality
of housing is poor. Much of the
housing in the Netherlands and
Germany, for example, has higher
space standards. This can be partly
attributed to the culture of research
and development that exists in these
countries. The lessons from BedZED
should be absorbed and transferred to
new UK developments.

Mont Cenis Training Centre
Jourda & Perraudin
Herne-Sodingen
Germany
1997

→
The dynamic skin of
Mont Cenis acts as a
climatic filter.

In 1991 a competition was organized jointly by IBA Emscher Park and Land Nordrhein–Westphalia in Herne-Sodingen, Germany, for a government training centre including seminar facilities, meeting rooms, hotel-type accommodation, a restaurant, a gymnasium, a library and leisure facilities including sports fields. The two-stage competition was won by architects Jourda & Perraudin from Lyons, France.

As far back as 1980, Jourda & Perraudin had been exploring the idea of an architecture in which different climatic zones in a building would provide different comfort conditions to match particular activities.[1] The idea of a house within a house – similar in concept to a Russian doll – has been a constantly recurring theme in their work, and the competition entry for the German academy was rooted in this tradition.

In 1993 Jourda & Perraudin with consulting engineers Arup Partners and Agibat MTI completed a research project under the Joule II programme of the European Union Directorate General XII based on the design strategy of 'a microclimatic envelope'. Their conclusions were that real environmental benefits might accrue from an envelope of this kind. Further proposals were added to incorporate approximately 10,000m^2 (107,600ft^2) of photovoltaic cells to act as a solar-power generator integrated with the roof of the envelope. The original competition brief was modified to include a public library, a multi-purpose hall and local authority offices.

A new company, EMC (Entwicklungsgesellschaft Mont Cenis), was founded to represent the various client bodies, and construction began in 1997. That year, the design was exhibited in the German pavilion at the Architecture Biennial in Venice and at the world conference for

→

CFD study of chilled
ceiling displacement
(typical internal
office).

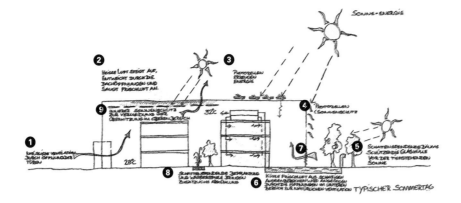

Typical summer's day

1 Doors open for views and
  natural ventilation
2 Hot air rises and escapes through
  open rooflights, drawing fresh air
  in at low level
3 Solar water heater
4 Photovoltaic cells (solar shades)
5 Trees shade glasshouse from
  low-angle sun
6 Cool fresh air drawn in from
  shade areas outside glasshouse
7 Low-level openings from
  natural ventilation
8 Vegetation and water features
  shade and evaporatively cool
  glasshouse
9 Internal shades trap solar heat
  at high level

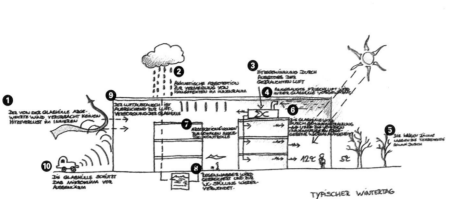

Typical winter's day

1 Wind, deflected by glasshouse,
  minimizes wind heat losses from
  the inner building
2 Acoustic absorption to limit
  glasshouse reverberation
3 Heat reclaimed from
  exhausted air
4 Fresh air drawn in and preheated
  by glasshouse
5 Trees shed leaves, allowing in
  low-angle sun
6 Glasshouse heated by sun and
  heat loss from buildings
7 Absorption 'cloud' for local
  acoustic control
8 Rainwater stored and reused
  to flush toilets
9 Infiltration rate sufficient to keep
  glasshouse fresh
10 Glasshouse protects
   microclimate from outside noise

environmental protection in Kyoto, and the building was completed in 1999. It is ground-breaking in its use of the microclimatic envelope to provide environmental comfort with large-scale energy savings.

Location

Herne is situated in the heart of the Ruhr, an area traditionally dominated by heavy industry, which has become a focus for urban and economic regeneration. The town of Sodingen – once dominated by the coal mine at Mont Cenis, now closed and demolished – is the site for the new development, which is part of the International Bauausstellung Emscher Park (International Architecture Exhibition).

The project aims to be a beacon for regeneration in the area, not only socio-economically but also

environmentally – by developing a redundant and contaminated mine site and using new clean-energy sources and bioclimatic building. The development has five main elements:

· an education centre for the minister of the interior of Nordrhein-Westphalia
· municipal buildings including a multi-purpose meeting hall, a civic administration building and a library
· new shops, public services and offices connected to an existing shopping centre
· 250 units of housing extended from the neighbouring area
· a landscaped park

Urban context

The strategy was to convert the former mine site into parkland, which

would be linked in the south to the existing town centre and in the north to the open green space of Vosshacken. Also to the north is a square bordered by an extension to an existing shopping centre.

A set of steps lined on both sides by buildings leads up to the park from the town centre. At the head of the steps is the academy, planned as a conspicuous landmark, with the education centre – the heart of the project – located in an oval clearing. To the east is a car park accessible from Kirchstrasse. The housing can be reached by the same route, and at the end of the main axis lies the Belvedere, a geometric form created from demolition waste. The contaminated land to the north has been drained by a network of trenches and embankments, and planted. Raised wooden walkways will form

← Cross-section.

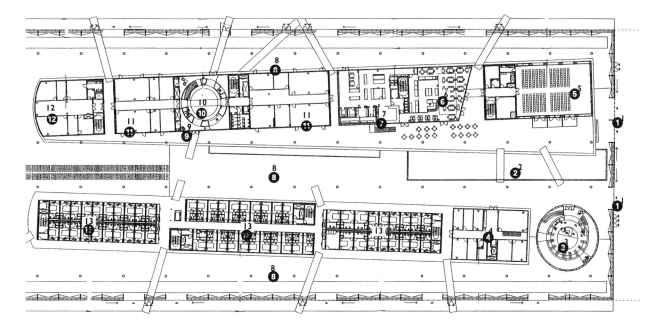

← Site plan.

1   Main public entrance
2   Pool
3   Library
4   Municipal offices
5   Multi-purpose hall
6   Café
7   Recreational facilities
8   Winter garden
9   Training Centre
10 Reception
11 Classrooms
12 Training Centre offices
13 Residential
    accommodation

part of a new public square on previously inaccessible land.

Form

The concept of the microclimatic envelope consists of a glazed 'blanket' thrown over a group of buildings to create a controlled environment between the buildings. The interior of the envelope is characterized by a temperate climate protected from rain and wind, making it a more attractive setting for social activities. In Herne-Sodingen the buildings are grouped in two blocks around a communal space. The zone between the microclimatic envelope and the buildings links occupied spaces with the landscape and surrounding park, making it a spatial as well as a climatic buffer between inside and outside.

The glass envelope is therefore the scene of a climatic shift – the buffer

space is climatically Mediterranean rather than northern European. This has had a 'knock-on' effect in the design of the buildings contained by the envelope, which have been effectively re-sited to a more temperate climate. In summer, parts of the façade can be opened to improve ventilation. The vegetation and the water basin contribute to summer cooling in the buffer zone, while the interiors of the buildings are cooled and ventilated by air drawn through tunnels.

Layout

Within the microclimatic envelope lies a new urban village offering community, educational and leisure amenities. The buildings are a collection of rational, cool, almost neutral timber boxes placed within the envelope; they are arranged in two

long blocks tilted towards one another to force a long perspective to the park to the north. At the centre of the complex is the academy, a three-storey lineal block dominated by a glazed entrance in the form of a three-storey toplit conical column containing reception, stairs and meeting rooms. Beyond this area is a series of flexible classrooms arranged in six zones on either side of a central circulation spine. Opposite the academy is a hotel consisting of three blocks, each of three levels arranged lineally on a deck. The two end blocks can be accessed directly from this galleried deck, made possible by the climatic modification of the envelope. The central block is more traditionally served by a central corridor, with hotel rooms each side.

The civic accommodation is placed close to the main entrance at the

The timber structure is reminiscent of Victorian boat building sheds.

Detail of column head.

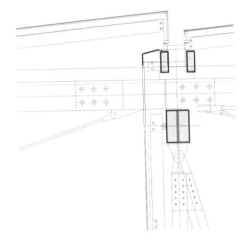

southern end of the hotel wing. This also consists of a three-storey block of mainly cellular rooms served by a central corridor. Also at the southern end of the academy wing is the public meeting room, a large versatile space used for receptions, meetings, shows and banquets; the southern elevation is fully glazed to provide visual contact with the town. The restaurant opens onto a landscaped deck on the ground floor sandwiched between the public meeting room and the academy. Located above the restaurant are a gymnasium, a sauna and a terrace. In the same way that the meeting hall punctuates the academy wing, the library – accessible from the public entrance in the south façade – punctuates the hotel wing. The library's conical shape makes it stand out when seen through the glazed envelope. It contains library

documentation for the education centre and the town and is intended to be a more enclosed and meditative space.

Structure and construction
The structure of the microclimatic envelope is a striking timber-column and lattice-beam hall reminiscent of great Victorian structures such as boat-building sheds and exhibition halls. As at the Crystal Palace, the principles of repetition have been applied for ease of construction. Primary and secondary structural grids are constant and allow for economical construction with an emphasis on prefabrication. The primary columns are made of trunks of pinewood from local renewable sources and their trunk-like shape has been maintained. Some of the buildings are made of reinforced

concrete, and the thermal mass acts as a balancing factor between differences in daytime and night-time temperatures. The repetitive 1.2/2.4m (4/8 ft), 12m and 24m (40ft and 80ft) module contribute to waste minimization.

Energy use and the microclimatic envelope
As well as providing shelter from the wind and rain, the envelope reduces overall energy consumption. In comparison with other similar buildings of the same insulation, a 23 per cent energy saving is predicted. There will also be a 28 per cent reduction in carbon dioxide emissions. The heating system will use less than 50KWh/m²/year (15,850 Btu/f²/annum) and the total energy consumption is predicted to be approximately 32KWh/m²/year (10,144

↑
The building complex
makes a dramatic
landmark at night-time.

Btu/f²/annum) when the system is at maximum use.[2]

Ventilation and thermal insulation
In winter, wind is deflected by the envelope and heat loss from the buildings is minimized. Fresh air is preheated by solar gain in the glasshouse and drawn into the buildings. The infiltration rate is controlled to keep the 'buffer zone' fresh. An air-handling unit with a heat exchanger has been installed to reclaim and redistribute heat from exhaust air. In summer, the doors of the envelope can be opened to promote natural ventilation; warm air rises and is vented through open roof vents, and cooler fresh air is drawn in at low level. The great glass roof is predominantly shaded by photovoltaic cells, while the walls are protected by trees, thereby avoiding excessive solar gains even on the warmest days.

Daylight
The envelope has been carefully designed to provide appropriate levels of daylight throughout the buffer zone and in the interiors of the buildings. The roof was designed as a cloud canopy simulating optimal sky conditions. Photovoltaic cells were arranged in varying density over the roof to provide shade in the appropriate spaces. Light shelves are incorporated into certain façades of the buildings to enable daylight penetration to deep spaces, and the two truncated cones of the library have a holographic film incorporated into the roof glazing to direct daylight by means of heliostat effects. A rainbow effect is created in the entrance hall.

Energy sources
The glazed roof of the building incorporates 8,400m² (90,380ft²) of photovoltaic cells within the 12,600m² (135,580ft²) total roof area. This generates a 1MW solar-power generation station. Arranged in cloud patterns, the modules provide optimal shading and protection from glare and direct solar gains. The density of the photovoltaic cells per panel varies from 58 per cent to 86 per cent, and energy production varies accordingly. Solar panels are also incorporated as shading into the west façade of the envelope. The total installation generates far in excess of the 750,000 KWh that the building demands; 600 inverters transform the DC current to AC current, and surplus energy can be fed back to the general grid. As well as the solar power, a number of other energy sources are integrated into the

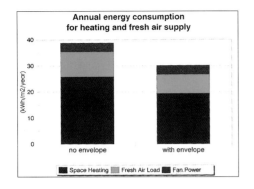

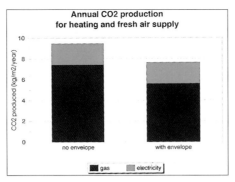

←

Comparative studies
of energy use and CO₂
production.

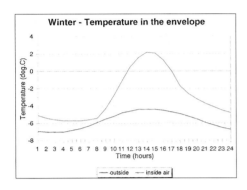

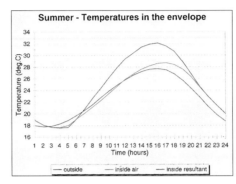

←

Modelling the effect
of temperatures in the
envelope.

←

Daylight studies to
ensure the daylight
penetration of training
spaces.

complex. The colliery pits release more than 1 million m³ (1,308,000yd³) of gas per year, 60 per cent of which is methane; the gas is used to fuel two co-generation units, producing both electricity and heat. The heat is used not only for the academy but also for the houses and a nearby hospital. Harnessing the excess gas from the disued colliery means that carbon dioxide emissions into the atmosphere are reduced by 12,000 tonnes (11,800 tons).

Conclusion

The development of the microclimatic envelope in the work of Jourda & Perraudin has reached its logical conclusion at Herne. Achieving a climatic shift by sheltering a collection of buildings – almost a civic precinct with a diverse range of occupancies – huge energy savings have been achieved. However, apart from the energy issues, the complex at Herne suggests a new kind of communal living – all under one roof. The notion of an 'in-between' hybrid space is not new, but has been neglected, if not forgotten. At Herne the roof admits daylight but also provides solar shading and is a solar collector; the walls supply the inhabitants with air, light and shade, making the envelope more of a climatic filter than an umbrella.

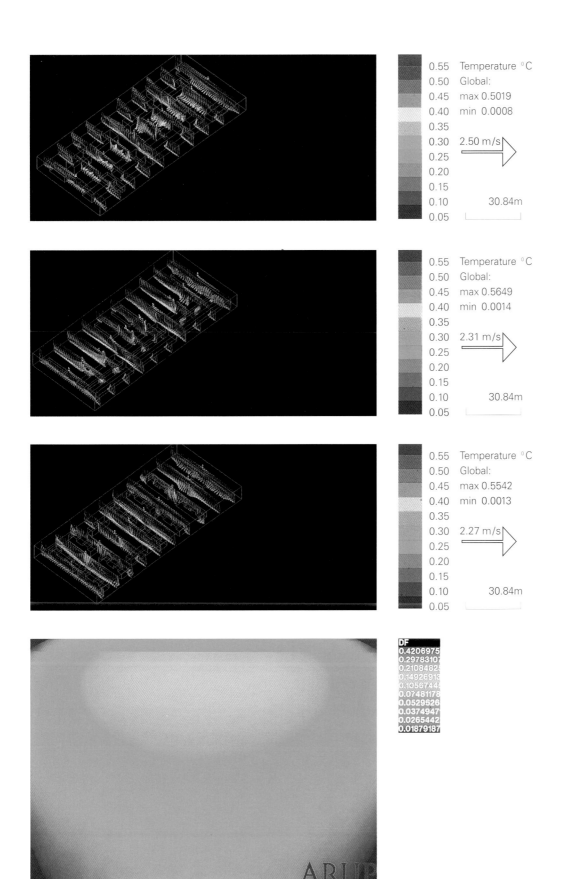

0.55   Temperature °C
0.50   Global:
0.45   max 0.5019
0.40   min 0.0008
0.35
0.30   2.50 m/s
0.25
0.20
0.15
0.10   30.84m
0.05

0.55   Temperature °C
0.50   Global:
0.45   max 0.5649
0.40   min 0.0014
0.35
0.30   2.31 m/s
0.25
0.20
0.15
0.10   30.84m
0.05

0.55   Temperature °C
0.50   Global:
0.45   max 0.5542
0.40   min 0.0013
0.35
0.30   2.27 m/s
0.25
0.20
0.15
0.10   30.84m
0.05

DF
0.4206975
0.29783107
0.21084825
0.14926913
0.10567444
0.07481178
0.05296926
0.0374947
0.0265442
0.01879187

← CFD studies were used to analyze an internal environment under different external conditions.

← Daylight studies of the glazed roof.

Interior showing photovoltaic shading of roof.

Varying density of photovoltaics to simulate cloud canopy.

The envelope creates a 'climatic' shift.

Jeremy Dixon and Edward Jones

Cambridge, UK

1994

→
View from the
south-east, across
the mill pool of the
River Cam.

The collegiate system of education practised in the ancient universities of Oxford and Cambridge enjoys a particular relationship with its architecture. In the historic colleges a particular morphology has evolved in which the principal elements of the college are organized around open courtyards – referred to as 'quads' at Oxford and 'courts' at Cambridge. In one way or another each college adopts and adapts this form to organize both the general spaces of students' living accommodation and the highly specific spaces of chapel, dining hall, master's lodging and, as

perhaps the most significant expression of the institution's scholarship, the library.

Darwin College, the first college in Cambridge exclusively for post-graduate students, was founded as recently as 1965. Its very modernity and its particular constitution make it distinctive within the long history and traditions of the university, and this is inevitably reflected in its architecture. At its foundation Darwin was expected to be a small college, with some 20 fellows and 40 or 50 students. Its chosen site was a beautiful but small area close to the

city centre, set between two busy roads and the river. Three existing houses, two of which had been in the ownership of the Darwin family, were joined together and enlarged by the construction of new buildings. This resulted in a linear arrangement in which the buildings acted as a buffer between the roads and the tranquillity of the garden and its river frontage. Within this plan the college put priority on providing residential accommodation for students, and it was decided to do without a chapel and a master's lodging, but a new dining hall was constructed and a

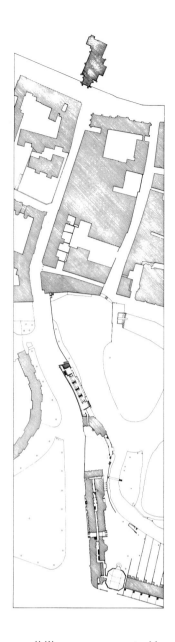

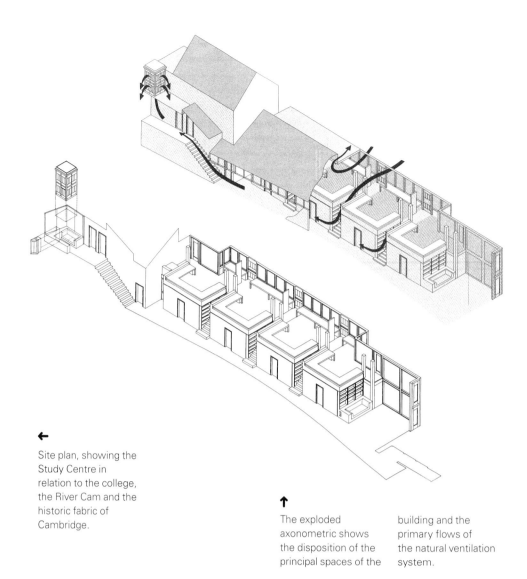

← Site plan, showing the Study Centre in relation to the college, the River Cam and the historic fabric of Cambridge.

↑ The exploded axonometric shows the disposition of the principal spaces of the building and the primary flows of the natural ventilation system.

small library was created by adapting two rooms in one of the existing houses.

In the last decades of the 20th century post-graduate study grew exponentially in British universities. By the late 1980s Darwin had more than 300 students from over 50 countries researching the entire range of academic disciplines. This put pressure on the central facilities and, in particular, on the small library, leading the college to explore the prospect of building a larger library to meet the demand for space and of providing students with access to IT facilities. Within the limitations of the small site there was only one possible location for the new building – a long, narrow piece of land wedged between a boundary wall and the river that had been the Darwin family's kitchen garden. This was the challenge that

faced the architects Jeremy Dixon and Edward Jones when they won a competition for the design of the building.

Site and programme

The site is 45m (148ft) long and varies in width between 6m (20ft) and 8m (26ft). Silver Street to the north is one of the few routes into the city centre over the River Cam, which it crosses by means of a bridge designed by Edwin Lutyens. Next to the site for the new building is the set-down point for the fleets of tourist buses that descend on Cambridge throughout the year. The river frontage, orientated slightly east of due south, looks across a wide millpond to Laundress Green, an open space much used in the summer by picnickers, that leads on to an area of open common lining the river.

The brief acknowledged that it would be impossible for an ordinary college library to satisfy the specialized needs of postgraduate students working in many different subject areas. At Darwin the aim is to provide a wide range of standard works of reference, guides, maps, critical and cultural works, particularly of an interdisciplinary nature, and major works of fiction. A tradition has been established for members of the college to donate copies of any books they write. One major element of the collection is the entire library of a former master, Sir Moses Finley, who bequeathed his unique collection of works – principally, but not exclusively, on ancient history – to the college. The college wanted to create a building that was more a place for private study than a store for books. In some cases the medium would be the

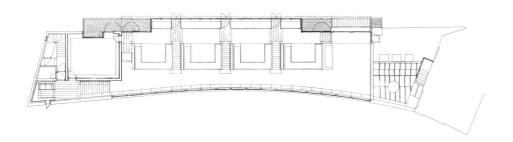

← Upper floor plan, showing the open-plan, principal study area.

↑ The river elevation of the new building extends and transforms the language of the 19th-century Old Granary by J.J. Stevenson.

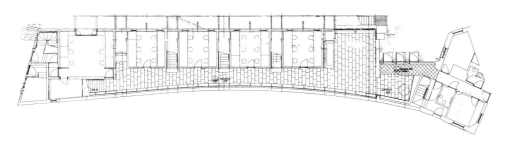

← The ground plan shows the cellular arrangement of the computer rooms.

book and the notepad; in more and more cases it would involve IT. A final element of the brief was to provide a flat for a research fellow.

Environmental synthesis

Any new building in the core of a historic city such as Cambridge carries obligations to its setting, so the form and language of the building are very specific to its site and programme. The site is at a major point of entry to the city, both by road over Lutyens' bridge and by river, where the bridge acts as a portal to the lyrical reach of the Cam known as 'the backs'. Within Darwin College grounds the site is immediately adjacent to a building known as 'the old granary', a former granary building converted in the 19th century into a dwelling for the Darwin family by J. J. Stevenson, a leading light of the so-called Queen Anne

Movement in architecture.

These facts, along with the dimensional constraints of the site, clearly influenced the arrangement of the building. But architectural invention is not purely a matter of mechanical response to constraint. What matters is the interpretation that is placed upon the facts. In this case a long, sloping roof rises from the northern boundary along the street towards the warmth of the southerly prospect across the river; this keeps the hostile street at bay and offers the possibility of creating a rich and diverse environment in which to study.

The cross-section places an expressed and expressive oak-framed structure above a solid brick-built base. A gently curved former garden wall has been reconstructed as a barrier to the street and to act within

the building as the principal location for book stacks. At the lower level, four enclosed rooms contain the fixed computer terminals. Above these and projecting above the river is a continuous but subtly differentiated study space which is covered in part by the bowed form of the sloping roof and, at its edge above the river, by a low flat ceiling.

The building is lit from a range of windows looking across the river and two clerestories, one to the south below the apex of the roof, the other sitting above the boundary wall to the north. A dynamic natural light suffuses the interior, its quality varying from room to room and changing with the seasons and the time of day. Rippling reflections from the river play across the ceiling of the study space. At the point of entry into the building, the full dimension and

anatomy of the cross-section is revealed in a tall space filled with light from an enormous floor-to-ceiling window flanked by a large reading table. At the eastern end of the slender plan there is a three-storey brick block that at ground level has another computer room; above is a seminar room lined with bookcases containing Sir Moses Finley's library. The top floor houses the fellow's flat.

The sweeping range of bookcases that lines the wall to the street leads to a flight of stairs ascending to the seminar room on the first floor. At the head of the flight is a small private study space with an elegant leather seat. There is a rooflight at the top of an oak-lined lantern and a small window gives a view of the street outside – but neither of these is quite what it appears. Upon close examination, the window reveal is found to house an inclined mirror showing a view, not of the buildings of Queens' College directly across the street, but along the flank of the building towards the city centre. The rooflight lantern is similarly complex, embodying an essential element of the building's environmental control systems. The lantern's solid walls are in fact a series of mechanically operated flaps that can provide summer ventilation to the entire open volume of the study space.

Arup's environmental control strategy is based on a set of precise relationships between the form and materials of the building and relatively simple mechanical systems. The building is sealed from the noise and fumes of the coach stop in the street. The clerestory window that runs above the bookcases is triple-glazed with no opening lights. People using the library can open the south-facing windows above the continuous desk in the main study space to provide local ventilation. The south-facing clerestory opens automatically, in tandem with the vents of the timber lantern. This promotes cross and linear ventilation through the building, drawing fresh air from over the river. The mechanisms respond to temperature, wind speed and rain. A computer simulation model was used to test the effectiveness of this passive system at the design stage. Heating for the main body of the building is supplied by radiators located under the windows and underfloor heating beneath the limestone floor of the book-lined gallery on the ground floor. The computer rooms have different environmental requirements from those of the open study space. These are lit by relatively small

← The structural and environmental logic of the building are expressed in the cross-sectional view from the entrance.

↑ The reconstructed garden wall becomes the northern face of the building. The oak ventilation box is a major element of the composition.

→ Readers enjoy visual contact with activity on the river.

windows giving views of the river, so the architects had to provide adequate background lighting while avoiding reflections in computer screens. The rooms have local fan-coil heating and cooling devices, which means they can be closed off from the general space to contain noise from keyboards and printers.

The building's artificial lighting is a subtle combination of low-level background illumination and focused pools of light emanating from the individual desk lamps that punctuate the work surfaces and establish individual territories within the collective space. This arrangement is another example – one of many found throughout the building – of the thoughtful analysis that has been made of users' needs.

Conclusion

In addition to producing an enjoyable environment for study, the building unobtrusively demonstrates an understanding of the principles of low-energy design. Its well-insulated envelope minimizes heat loss and the asymmetry of the cross-section differentiates between the conditions to north (relatively hostile) and south (relatively benign). The structural form is precisely related to the environmental strategy.

The principles that inform the environmental design of Darwin college library are very simple. They are not far removed from those that might be found in a house designed by one of the leading architects of the Arts and Crafts Movement. Indeed, the observance of the difference between a northerly and a southerly aspect is one of the defining characteristics of houses by C. F. A.

Voysey, M. H. Baillie Scott and their contemporaries. But, compared with what may be appropriate in a house, a late 20th-century academic library, or 'study centre', demands a more predictable and controllable environmental system.

The achievement of the designers, architects and engineers of the Darwin building is that its synthesis – achieved with apparent effortlessness – is based on quite sophisticated architectural science. The building is quite small, no bigger than many Arts and Crafts houses, and is the product of a unique set of circumstances. It nonetheless stands as a potent example of how architecture and engineering can collaborate in responding to the challenges of the new environmental agenda.

112

←
The principal study
space inhabits the
oak roof structure
and is illuminated
and ventilated by the
continuous
clerestory.

↑
From the south-west,
the glazed, timber-
framed reading areas
wrap around and
overhang the
masonry base.

Jubilee Campus University of Nottingham

Michael Hopkins & Partners

Nottingham, UK

2000

→

The learning resources
centre at Nottingham
University's Jubilee
Campus is a free-
standing inverted
cone.

In 1996 the University of Nottingham held a design competition for a proposed Jubilee Campus to commemorate the university's 50th anniversary. The campus was envisaged as a model for sustainable development in the East Midlands and as an example of the affordable and sustainable regeneration of a former industrial site. The limited competition involved top UK architects in the field of design for higher education and sustainability (including Feilden Clegg and Macormac Jamieson & Pritchard). The architects Michael Hopkins & Partners were appointed with Ove Arup & Partners as services and structural engineer and Battle McCarthy as landscape architect.

The brief for the campus consisted of 41,000m² (441,160ft²) of buildings including undergraduate and postgraduate accommodation, three faculty buildings, a central teaching building and a learning resources centre. Nottingham University is among a group of postwar institutions that grew from previous university college status and expanded again in the 1960s. It has been described as a place where 'Basil Spence's progressive, but eclectic Modernism co-existed with the Banker's Georgian

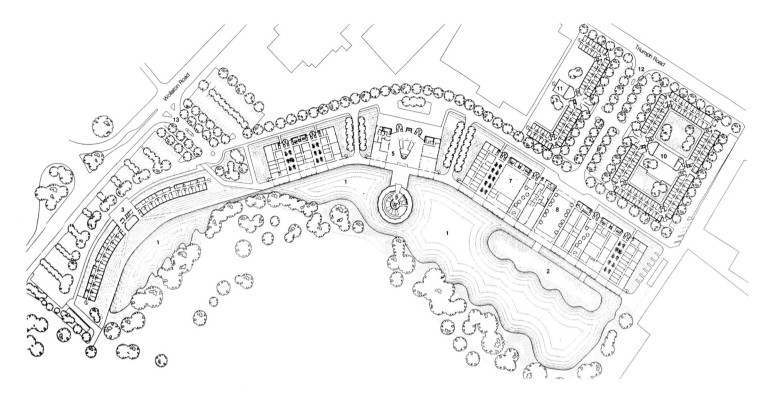

Site layout.

1 Lake	6 Learning Resource	9 Departments of	11 Undergraduate
2 Grassed island	Centre	Education / Higher	Halls
3 Postgraduate Hall	7 Department of	Education	12 Entrance
4 Business School	Computer Science	10 Undergraduate	13 Main entrance
5 Central Teaching	8 Central Catering	Halls	
Facility	Facility		

of Morley Horder and Cecil Howitt'. [1]

The building type developed at Nottingham over the period since its Royal Charter and before can be called pavilions set within a romantic landscape. Hopkins's competition entry responds to and builds on this typology of pavilions in a parkland; it also builds on the Inland Revenue buildings by the same architects and engineers less than a mile from the proposed new campus.

Site location and layout

About 1.6km (1 mile) away from its existing Beeston Campus, the university secured a 7.5ha (18½ acre) 'brownfield' site, where a Raleigh bicycle factory once stood, set between an industrial zone and interwar suburban housing. The centre point of the proposal is a 13,000m² (139,880ft²) linear lake that

forms a buffer between the new campus and the housing. As well as providing waterside promenades and reintroducing wildlife to the area, the lake echoes the use of water on the main campus.

Pedestrian movement is given priority over cars by containing parking and traffic to the north. Buildings are sited to exploit views over the lake and to benefit from the possibilities of passive design. Teaching and social spaces face west and south-west. Student residences are treated differently, with undergraduate halls taking the more familiar quadrangle form (although, unlike Oxford and Cambridge, they are served by corridors rather than stairs), whereas the postgraduate accommodation snakes along the side of the lake, recalling Alvar Aalto's halls of residence at MIT.

The entrance to the site is flanked by the undergraduate halls of residence and trees, making a formal avenue, again echoing the city of Nottingham. At the end of the avenue is the transparent three-storey refectory, allowing glimpses through to the lake beyond, which is flanked by teaching pavilions lining the banks of the lake. These pavilions effectively contain the park to the west of the lake and are also based on a typology. Rational corridor-served blocks contain either closed or open atria. Views from the teaching pavilions are therefore varied – either into the atria or across the lake and into the park. The pavilions are interspersed with places of high-intensity student activity, including the refectory and the central teaching facility, which contains a number of lecture theatres stacked vertically within an atrium flanked by facilities such as a bank, a

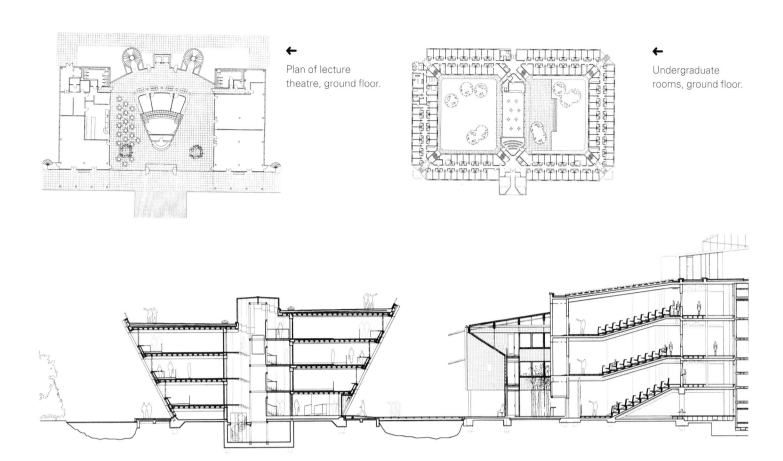

←
Plan of lecture
theatre, ground floor.

←
Undergraduate
rooms, ground floor.

↑
Section through
learning resources
centre and lecture
theatres.

shop and students' union meeting rooms.

Sited opposite the learning resources centre, the central teaching facility is the only element in the whole composition that has been allowed to break free from the banks of the lake and occupy a peninsula jutting out into it. The functional dialogue between the two elements of the campus seems more appropriate than the formal one. The learning resources centre takes the form of an inverted polygonal cone intended to provide panoramas over the lake. Whereas the largest lecture theatre in the central teaching facility is placed at the top of the stack and the smallest at ground level in order minimize the footprint in the public atrium, the form of the learning resources centre is less rooted in the rationale of the campus and appears

to be perched rather uncomfortably on its promontory.

Structure and materials

The structure for the teaching pavilions is simple and straightforward. In-situ concrete floors are supported by columns on a 6m by 6m grid, exposed to provide thermal mass. External envelopes are designed to be thermally efficient and made of materials from sustainable sources. Roofs, for example, are green and are planted with tundra species, giving a U value of 0.22 W/m^2/°C (0.04 Btu/h/ft^2/°F). Faculty buildings are clad predominantly in western red cedar from a Canadian source chosen because it holds WWF/FSC certification. These prefabricated timber panels cloak a layer of cellulose Warmcell insulation incorporated into a breathing wall construction with a U

value of 0.287 W/m^2/°C (0.05 Btu/h/ft^2/°F). The overall performance of the walls and the low maintenance costs of the cladding helped to persuade the initially sceptical client of the suitability of the timber as a cladding. Cedar is also used in the interior of the atria, where panels incorporate a layer of hessian-covered quilt to ensure acceptable acoustic qualities. The timber will weather to a silver colour over time – the exterior long before the interior.

Prefabricated cladding panels and windows are framed in hot-dipped galvanized steel, a material that is also used for the glazed elements of atria and walkways. As well as being a cheaper alternative to stainless steel, the galvanized steel was considered by the architects to be more eco-friendly. Motorized retractable fabric blinds – which animate and enliven

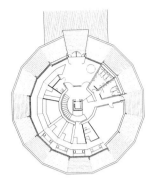

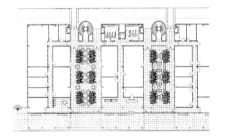

Roof-mounted cowl.

The central teaching facility.

the building forms and help to reduce fabric temperatures and shade windows – relieve this spare and perhaps austere palette of materials.

Energy and environment
Although the original competition brief specified that buildings should be low-energy and naturally ventilated 'wherever possible', the design team did not find it too prescriptive. The three faculty buildings – dedicated to education, computer science, and management and finance – appeared to offer the main opportunities for low-energy services. Arup's previous collaborations with the Hopkins office at the Inland Revenue building in Nottingham, the Saga Headquarters in Folkestone and Portcullis House, Westminster, provided models for an elementary low-pressure ventilation

system. This was augmented by Arup's own European Union-funded research into solar and wind energy and wind-tunnel testing of alternative chimney terminals.

Ventilation
Background data suggested that low-pressure mechanical ventilation geared to heat recovery would provide a more energy-efficient system than natural ventilation. The system is predicted to operate in this mode for the majority of the year but windows can be controlled to enable the building to be entirely naturally ventilated by stack effect.

In the mixed mode, air is drawn into air-handling units mounted at roof level, where it is filtered electrostatically and blown through vertical air ducts into floor voids, where it is delivered into teaching

rooms through low-pressure floor diffusers at a rate of 2.5 l/s (0.089 ft³/s) for each square metre (11ft²) of room space. Exhaust air is returned using the corridor as the extract path. Acoustic separation is maintained through the use of a low-pressure attenuated floor path between teaching rooms and the corridor. From the corridor the air is drawn into the stairwell and returned to the atria for heat recovery or evaporative cooling – or extracted through the roof cowls.

A key feature of the low-energy mechanical system is that fan power is minimized through pressure drops. Ducts, which must be as large as possible to reduce air pressure, lead into floor voids and carry air with velocities as low as 1.5 m/s (4.92 ft/s). Floor voids are also larger than standard, with a 350mm (14in) deep void. The plant is equipped with a

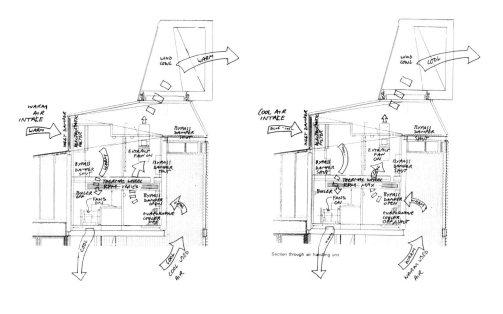

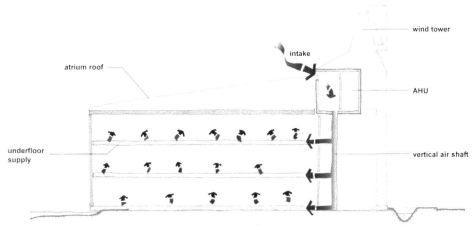

← Supply air and extract air routes. Air intake is through the roof-mounted AHHs via a thermal wheel. It is then blown through vertical ducts into the floor void. Exhaust air returns through the stairwell to the AHU for heat recovery or evaporative cooling and is expelled via the cowl.

↑ The roof-mounted cowls.

sophisticated bypass system so that components that create pressure drops, such as the evaporative humidifier, can be eliminated when not in use. Arup designed a balanced flue boiler for the system, instead of a heating coil that would again create a pressure drop.

Efforts to reduce pressure drop have paid off in that the fans now deal with pressures from 28 to 34 Pa depending on season (a conventional system deals with 1200 Pa to 1600 Pa). Mechanical ventilation will probably be used for much of the year, but natural ventilation is possible by opening windows to admit fresh air and stack effect for exhaust though the stairwell chimney.

The steel cowls that punctuate the roof forms, located above the modular air-handling units, are designed to revolve and turn in the wind so that the exhaust vents always face downwards, thereby maintaining extraction of exhaust air. They also reflect a desire to add a finishing touch, in the form of a bonnet, to the rather self-consciously 'green' uniform that the buildings wear. Indeed, this display of 'exposed power' is hardly merited – as the designers acknowledge, 'the reality of wind in suction mode provides only a very small force indeed'.[2] This mode of passive ventilation may operate when external temperatures are between 18°C (64°F) and 25°C (77°F).

The central teaching facility operates on the same principles as the main teaching blocks. There, however, air is cooled and delivered below lecture theatre seating. While the buildings will not be tested for air tightness ducts and floor voids have been pressure-tested to ensure that

infiltration rates are as predicted. The campus atria are single-glazed and unheated, and ventilation is independent and non-powered. Atria are designed with profiled nose-shaped south facades to promote natural ventilation.

Wind-tunnel tests demonstrated that the cowls would turn in wind speeds of as little as 2m/s (6.56ft/s) and were stable in winds in excess of 40m/s (131.23ft/s), but design figures indicate that the fan energy saved by using the cowl is less than 1 per cent of total fan power.

Ventilation fans are powered by a total area of 450m² (4,840ft²) of photovoltaic solar cells integrated into the atrium roofs. As well as providing 51,240 Wh of annual energy output, the four arrays of monocrystalline cells effectively shade the atrium roofs.

Construction process from the brownfield site of the campus.

450m² (4,840ft²) of pv cells are designed to match annual fan power.

Heating

Condensing gas boilers on the roof of each building deliver heat through standard radiators fitted with thermostatic valves. The heating system is sized to integrate with the cooling system and to take account of the beneficial effect of energy stored in thermal mass. Incoming fresh air is heated to 18°C (64°F) by being passed through thermal wheels. When external temperatures fall below 2.3°C (36°F) heating is supplemented by a 30KW gas-fired boiler mounted on the air-handling unit. Predictions, based on weather data for Nottingham, show that the boiler will be used for only 10 per cent of hours when the buildings are occupied.

Lighting

Daylight is used as the primary light source wherever possible. The teaching spaces are lit through ribbon windows; this is controlled by fixed horizontal louvres that cover the top halves of east- and west-facing windows. The white-coloured louvres and internal light shelves combine to reduce glare and produce even distribution of daylight across the room depths.

Toplighting is supplied in top-floor seminar rooms through light tubes. The electric lighting is controlled by a stand-alone intelligent lighting management system linked to passive infrared detectors in every room, and custom-made luminaires at the perimeter of rooms have daylight sensors, which switch and dim them depending on daylight levels.

Conclusion

Overall energy use is predicted to be two-thirds that of naturally ventilated cellular offices – but the Jubilee Campus displays its environmental credentials in other ways. Its palette of recognizably eco-friendly features includes green space, water and wildlife, plenty of timber, and green roofs topped with the almost mandatory chimneys. The buildings lean slightly away from the more neutral but highly crafted creations of Hopkins's traditional work. The overall result is interesting in the light of the current drive for efficiency, prefabrication and value for money in the UK construction industry. Mass customization meets William Morris at the Jubilee Campus. As Peter Fawcett comments, 'It generates a quintessentially English campus, free from the empty formal posturing, or equally techno-fetishism of his competitors.'[3]

←
Toplighting is used to daylight top-floor seminar rooms.

↑
Roof lighting.

→
Solar control to the learning resources centre.

←

Campus in use: the lakeside arcade has an appropriate scale and form.

Cultural Centre

Renzo Piano
Nouméa
New Caledonia
1997

→

The 'cases' of the
Nouméa complex.

'The return to tradition is a myth.... No people has ever achieved that. The search for identity, for a model, I believe it lies before us...our identity is before us.'[1] These words provide the inspiration for the design of a new cultural centre at Nouméa in New Caledonia. They belong to Jean-Marie Tjibaou, who was the leader of the New Caledonian independence movement. His vision for the people of New Caledonia to achieve a balance of their tradition with the modern world is paralleled in Renzo Piano's creation.

Piano appears to be one of a few living architects who can successfully face up to the challenge of cultural devaluation brought on by the 'all pervasive thrust of the media and the market'.[2] The work of the Renzo Piano Building Workshop is based on rigorously investigating the needs of people who use buildings and interpreting these through constructional discipline. This method, however, is always inflected by a contextual and cultural sensibility and the collaborative approach of the 'workshop'. The Nouméa design passed through a number of stages as the workshop studied, researched and reinterpreted the scheme. The result is a building which, though completely original,

↑
The buildings in the
'oceanic tropical'
setting.

↑
Typical Kanak huts –
inspiration for the
case forms.

evokes elements of traditional indigenous settlements and plant forms.

Before Tjibaou's death in 1989, at the hands of Kanak extremists who opposed the referendum on independence agreed with the French, it had already been decided to build a centre dedicated to Kanak culture. An international design competition, held in 1991 on behalf of the Agence de Développement de la Culture Kanak (ADCK), was won by the Renzo Piano Building Workshop, working with Arup. Given to ADCK by the municipality of Nouméa, the site was the place where Tjibaou had held the Melanesia 2000 festival in 1975 – one of the milestones in the struggle for political and cultural recognition.

Location and site
New Caledonia is an island in the Pacific Ocean approximately 1,600km (1,000 miles) east of Australia. The site is set on a promontory covered in palm and pine trees which separates the Bay of Magenta from a small lagoon on the eastern edge of Nouméa, the capital. The climate is 'oceanic tropical', meaning that it is generally humid throughout the year with only moderate variations in temperature.

A full annual weather record was recorded at Nouméa airport and analysed for temperature, humidity and wind speed and direction. The average winter minimum is 18°C (64°F) and the average summer minimum is 28°C (82°F). The relative humidity is very high at about 75 per cent, with average monthly maximums of 90 per cent and lows of 60 per cent. It is no easy task to provide comfort conditions using passive design in such a climate.

Design development
The competition design of April 1991 sought to establish the centre as part of the landscape and culture of New Caledonia by evoking vegetal analogies and formal echoes with traditional settlements both in plan and section.[3]

A covered promenade, curved like a stalk, was laid out on the crest of the promontory to link the various departments. The major spaces, circular in plan, were held inside shell-like elements made predominantly of timber. Tall, layered and curved, these were known as 'cases' and – in addition to their evocative connections to programme and place – were intended as primary means of shelter and climate modification. The cases relate formally and visually to, but do not mimic, the indigenous bush and Norfolk Island pine trees

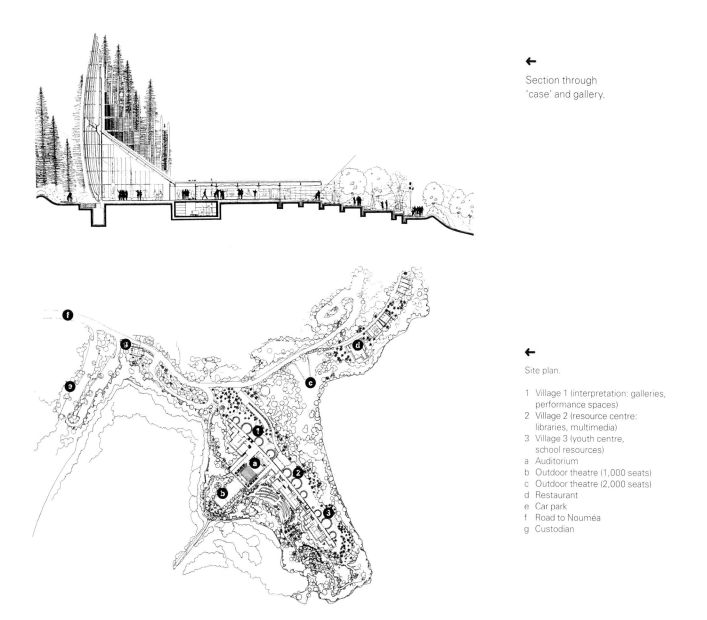

←

Section through
'case' and gallery.

←

Site plan.

1 Village 1 (interpretation: galleries,
   performance spaces)
2 Village 2 (resource centre:
   libraries, multimedia)
3 Village 3 (youth centre,
   school resources)
a Auditorium
b Outdoor theatre (1,000 seats)
c Outdoor theatre (2,000 seats)
d Restaurant
e Car park
f Road to Nouméa
g Custodian

and the traditional Kanak huts and settlements. They were also designed to promote natural wind-driven ventilation by directing and accelerating breezes into internal spaces and by setting up convective stack ventilation within the buildings. In the original competition design, the cases were placed on both sides of the curved promenade.

Access to the site is from the north and the access road skirts the lagoon to reach the promenade through a shaded car park before turning east towards a residential quarter for visiting artists. The area between the residential quarter and the cultural centre was planned to contain an arc of traditional huts with spaces between each – a showcase for traditional Kanak life and Kanak ceremonies. The constituent parts of the centre were located at appropriate

places along the promenade: public facilities close to the entrance, an auditorium and media theatre on the quiet lagoon side, a multi-purpose hall on the lagoon side, with a bar/cafeteria and lounge on the opposite side. This original zoning survived the development of the design but has been changed as the brief was modified.

Piano's cases are the most striking feature of the scheme. They are as tall as the surrounding pine trees (nearly 30m (98ft)) and were designed originally from a mixture of specially adapted local materials. Although reminiscent of the ribbed construction of Kanak huts, the cages are not a literal reinterpretation of the vernacular. They are much larger than the huts and are constructed of laminated iroko tied with stainless-steel tubes and rods. Therefore, while

the overall forms are traditional, the construction of the cases relies on innovation. Equivalent in height to ten-storey structures, they must be built to resist cyclonic and earthquake conditions. Not an indigenous timber, iroko was chosen on account of its strength and durability; it needs no decorative protection and weathers to a silver grey similar to that of the surrounding pines.

The layout of the scheme developed from the original competition entry. In the feasibility study of January 1992 the cases are grouped to resemble three separate village clusters and they are more sculptural than in their finally developed form. By January 1993 the flat roof had been swept up to become an integral part of the case, and the cases themselves had evolved into a double layer of laminated timber ribs.

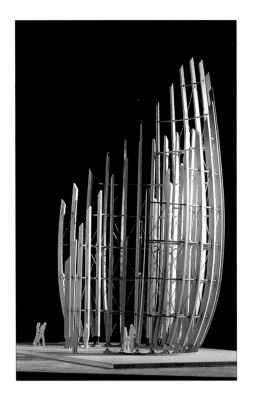

↑
Physical scale models
were used to test
form, scale and
construction.

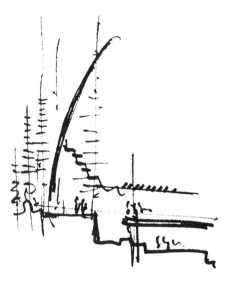

↑
Sketch of a 'case'.

↑
Part of a full-scale
'case' mock-up in
France.

The varying dimensions of the horizontal slatted cladding – widely spaced at the top and bottom, more narrowly spaced in the middle – were determined by the ventilation studies. The cases eventually detailed in April 1993 defined only about two-thirds of a circle on plan. They had also acquired straight sloping roofs of glass or metal. The cases had also been evenly spaced, and the original concept of the three villages becomes difficult to read.

The layout of the complex also changed from the original competition entry and early feasibility study, although the original zoning survives. Three groups of cases, or villages, are set along the southern side of a curved promenade. Village 1 contains interpretation galleries and performance spaces. Village 2 has a resources centre and libraries. Village

3 accommodates the youth centre and educational resources.

Structure and construction
Arup was responsible for the concept design and analysis up to tender stage, while the French company Agibat MTI took charge of formal design completion.

There are three sizes of cases all sharing a similar structure designed to resist cyclonic winds that can gust up to approximately 65m/s (213.25 ft/s) from any direction. The tallest case is 28m (92ft) high with an internal diameter of 14m (46ft). Structural and formal development was determined by wind conditions and passive ventilation mechanisms. In the final form, two concentric walls are set out from a common centre point. The structural elements of both skins consist of glue-laminated columns –

arched in the outer ring and straight in the internal ring. They are tied together and braced to provide overall wind resistance.

The timbers are braced with steel tubes placed at 2.25m (7ft) vertical centres with single diagonal ties in each bay, apart from the lower internal ring where opening windows are placed. To prevent distortions, the inner and outer walls are tied together with up to three levels of belt trusses; the sloping roof is designed to lie inside the inner walls, allowing the roof to be free from stresses from wall movements and also to be relatively lightweight. Connections were carefully considered to enable the cases to be externally skinned with horizontal slats; a steel casting is inserted into the timber columns accommodating compact fixings for diagonal steel rods.

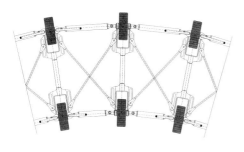

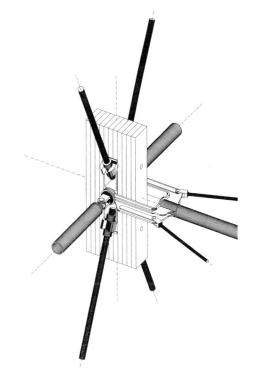

↑
Detail of paired ribs to
'case'.

↑
Void between two
skins.

↑
Timber construction
to bracing tubes and
diagonals.

The connection of the feet of the timber columns to concrete foundations is equally carefully and elegantly resolved. The choice of iroko for the structure was determined by a number of performance factors but durability was critical: humidity, maritime conditions, termite resistance and gluing characteristics were all taken into account.

The structure and construction, while unique, are products of the developmental and constructional discipline of the Renzo Piano Building Workshop. Material development stems from the timber technology developed by the architects on previous projects, eg. the IBM travelling exhibition. Similarly, structural relationships can be identified in a number of other projects, including the workshop's own offices and the envelope,

particularly the modular double roof, is another identifiable motif.

Energy and environment
The principal spaces are cocooned in circular cases connected along one edge by a circulation spine. Environmental conditions inside the spaces are protected and modified by the cases. The other side of the spine consists of pavilions with stainless-steel flat roofs supported on laminated iroko posts and beams. The cases are clad in horizontal iroko slats and the pavilions in glass and iroko louvres positioned and regulated to promote a passive ventilation system. In order to achieve natural wind-driven ventilation for a wide variety of wind speeds and directions, a five-stage control strategy was devised by Arup.

Louvres in the case of the building are opened and closed in response to

wind conditions. Several openings allow ventilation. Two face towards the prevailing winds; one opening is set 2m (6$\frac{1}{2}$ft) above ground, another 0.5m (1$\frac{1}{2}$ft) above ground. On the other side of the case, a series of openable windows allow for cross ventilation. The windows have three positions – open, closed or half closed – and are controlled automatically. The opening position is dependent on external wind speed and is open only enough to achieve internal air speeds to a maximum of 1.5m/s (4.92 ft/s).

Each case has a double-louvred opening at a high level; when this is open, the case can operate as a chimney, providing ventilation (through stack effect or natural ventilation) on days when wind-driven cross ventilation is impossible. On windy days, the curved form of the case directs the wind up and over the

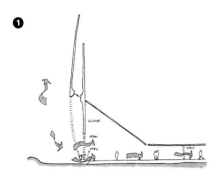

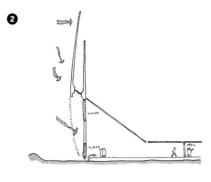

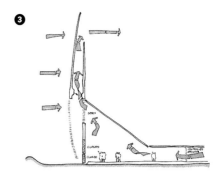

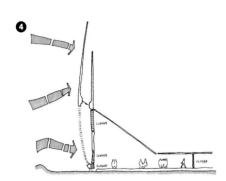

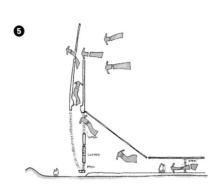

←

Various modes of
operation for openings
in the case.

1 Light winds
2 Moderate winds
3 Strong winds
4 Cyclonic conditions
5 Reverse winds

chimney, setting up a negative
pressure that draws air up and over
the chimney and pushes it through the
internal space from the louvred
openings on the opposite side of the
case. When the prevailing winds are
from an opposite direction, the
chimney acts in reverse. If a cyclone
occurs, the envelope is closed,
'battened and hatched'.

Prediction of comfort conditions
Comfort conditions were analysed by
means of the Arup Room program,
using weather data for the peninsula.
Air temperature, radiant temperature
and humidity were calculated for each
hour every day of the year at a
number of points in occupied spaces
for each of the control modes. This
information was supplemented with
information on how outside wind
conditions would generate air

movement in spaces. To accomplish
this, a 1:50 scale model was
constructed and wind-tunnel tested by
Arup and CTSB in Nantes. Internal air
velocity was predicted for each mode
of operation based on coefficients for
each location and wind direction
applied to the wind speed data.

This data was combined with
temperature and humidity
calculations to arrive at a comfort
index at each position and for each
hour during the critical months of the
year. The results were compared
against indices of comfort for people
living in naturally ventilated
conditions in a tropical climate. The
predictions showed that in February,
the hottest month, comfort criteria
were met for all but 5.8 per cent of the
time the building was occupied.

Conclusion
In 1992 Piano made a forthright
statement about the role of the
architect: 'Unless an architect is able
to listen to people and understand
them, he may simply become
someone who creates architecture for
his own fame and self-glorification
instead of doing the real work he has
to do…an architect must be a
craftsman. Of course any tools will do.
These days, the tools might include a
computer, an experimental model,
and mathematics. However, it is still
craftsmanship – the work of someone
who does not separate the work of the
mind from the work of the hand. It
involves a circular process that draws
you from an idea to a drawing, from a
drawing to an experiment, from an
experiment to a construction, and
from construction back to an idea
again. For me, this cycle is

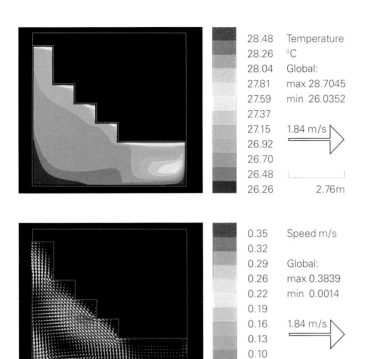

28.48	Temperature	
28.26	°C	
28.04	Global:	
27.81	max 28.7045	
27.59	min 26.0352	
27.37		
27.15	1.84 m/s	
26.92		
26.70		
26.48		
26.26	2.76m	

1.51	Speed m/s	
1.37		
1.23	Global:	
1.10	max 1.6423	
0.96	min 0.0046	
0.82		
0.69	8.40 m/s	
0.55		
0.41		
0.28		
0.14	2.76m	

0.35	Speed m/s	
0.32		
0.29	Global:	
0.26	max 0.3839	
0.22	min 0.0014	
0.19		
0.16	1.84 m/s	
0.13		
0.10		
0.07		
0.03	2.76m	

CFD analyses of air
speed and
temperature through
the case, in varying
conditions.

fundamental to creative work.
Unfortunately, many have come to
accept each of these steps as
independent.... Teamwork is essential
if creative projects are to come about.
Teamwork requires an ability to listen
and engage in a dialogue.'[4]

   This analysis describes precisely the
process of creating the Nouméa
cultural centre – a building that makes
a powerful contribution to Tjiabaou's
ambition to tell the work 'that we are
neither escapees from prehistory nor
archaeological remains, but men of
flesh and blood'.[5]

↑
Cultural and
contextual
sensitivity: the
complex from off-
shore.

→
Dining and library
facilities.

→

The complex at night:
the profile of the
cases is accentuated
by silhouetting.

Carmel Mountain Ranch Public Library

M.W. Steele Group Inc.
San Diego
California, USA
1996

➜

Detail of the structural
overhang.

With its mild winters and abundant sunshine, the climate of Southern California is most agreeable, in spite of atmospheric pollution in downtown areas – and the odd Hollywood downpour like the one Gene Kelly danced through at the highpoint of *Singing in the Rain*. The sequence of wonderful Californian houses that began with Greene and Greene – and continued through the work of Frank Lloyd Wright, Rudolf Schindler, Marcel Breuer and Richard Neutra up to the mid-20th century 'Case Study' houses by Craig Ellwood and Charles Eames – amply demonstrates how a happy synthesis of architecture and climate can be achieved there.[1] In all these buildings, form and fabric are organized to filter and moderate the ambient environment. Wide roof overhangs, widely opening doors and windows, shades and blinds, shaded terraces and patios are all part of the architectural and environmental language. Identical elements were found in other building types, for example, in a number of schools Neutra designed in the 1930s.

It was predictable that California should have been one of the first regions of the world where mechanical environmental control was adopted as the norm for buildings of all types. The influence of the aerospace industry and, more recently, of 'Silicon Glen', led to a predisposition for a technically based architecture. As explained in the

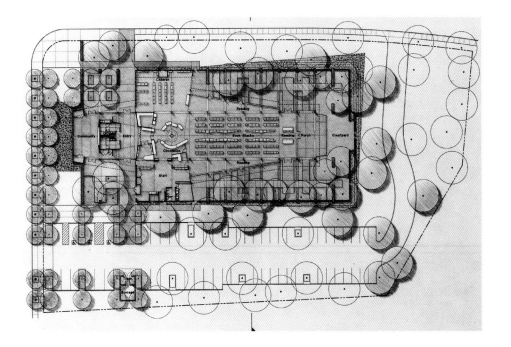

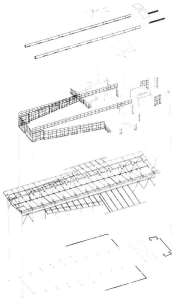

↑
Plan showing the
location of the library
within its walled
garden.

↑
Exploded
axonometric showing
the discrete systems
of structure,
enclosure and
services.

introduction, the 1960s SCSD schools programme, under the direction of Ezra Ehrenkrantz, was a symbol of this, bringing as it did the benefits of a fully air-conditioned, sealed environment to California's classrooms, in contrast with Neutra's earlier climate-filtering designs.

The design for Carmel Mountain Ranch Public Library by the M.W. Steele Group represents a return to California's environmental tradition in architecture. Working closely with Ove Arup & Partners California, M.W. Steele have produced a building that brings together that tradition with engineering systems in a functional relationship that seeks to combine the best of both worlds.

The library environment
The design of a public library, however small, is a rich architectural

challenge. In addition to its traditional function as a lending and reference source, a library is a place for private study by people of all ages and has also become an important point of access to digital information. Many people visit a library simply to borrow or return books and spend a relatively short time in the building. Others may spend many hours there working on projects, using books and/or digital sources of reference. There is often a separate children's section and many libraries provide a room, or rooms, for community use. Library staff, who spend all their working days in the building, have their own particular needs.

It would be possible to deal with these complex requirements in a simple environmental brief in which uniform and standardized levels of heat, light and sound are delivered

constantly throughout the building. Such a proposition was at the heart of the SCSD schools programme. Its advantage is precise environmental control regardless of the seasonal and diurnal variations in the natural world. But it is equally plausible to argue that the richness and diversity of a library's uses should be reflected in the provision of a diverse environment. This approach has been followed at Carmel Mountain Ranch and the whole character of the building flows from it.

Form and environment
The environment of the building ranges from the relatively stable conditions at the heart of the plan to the widely dynamic conditions of the tree-shaded courtyard that surrounds the main library space. The scissor-form roof structure and the newly

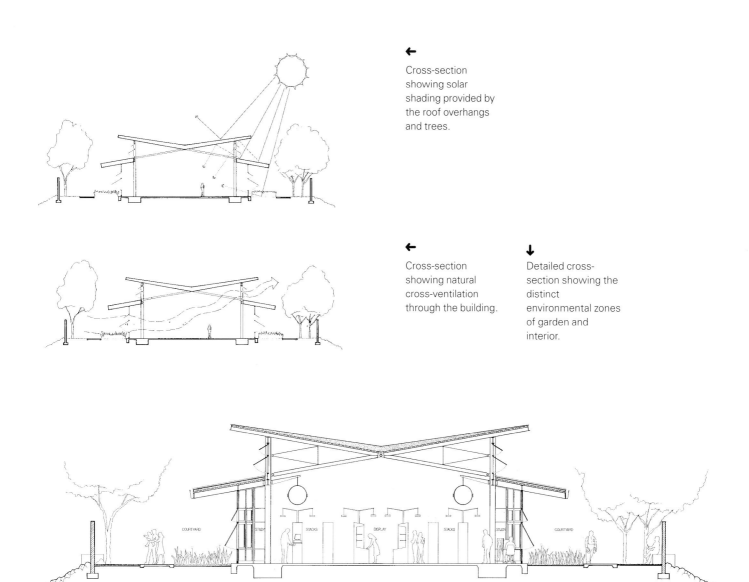

← Cross-section showing solar shading provided by the roof overhangs and trees.

← Cross-section showing natural cross-ventilation through the building.

↓ Detailed cross-section showing the distinct environmental zones of garden and interior.

planted trees create an almost continuous canopy, making the steel structure into a natural metaphor. In the 19th century Henri Labrouste adopted the same metaphor in his design for the reading room at the Bibliothèque Nationale in Paris, where the array of top-lit domes, supported on branching cast-iron columns, is a clear allusion to the luminous qualities of a forest glade – a point reinforced by the painted frieze of tree-tops around the perimeter of the room.

At Carmel Mountain Ranch the roof form is a direct expression of the environmental strategy. The primary mode of ventilation and cooling for the building is 'passive' or, in our terminology, 'selective'. Natural ventilation occurs through clerestory windows above the central 'nave' of the plan, and the wide eaves, which

overhang the main structure by 2.1m (7ft) provide shade for the windows in the heat of summer. At the perimeter, under the lower eaves of the aisle-like spaces, library visitors can open and close windows at will, but a small air-conditioning plant has been installed to provide 'peak trimming' of the temperature, either cooling or heating, in extreme conditions. The intention is to minimize energy consumption and running costs. The highly insulated roof deck reduces heat gain and the mass of exposed concrete floor slabs and dense masonry walls moderate internal temperature variations. Glazing provides a further degree of solar control. Plenty of daylight penetrates the building – the central bookstacks are lit from the clerestories and the reading areas from the windows that look out onto the courtyard. Energy-

efficient lamps, with automatic controls, supply artificial lighting at night.

The courtyard garden was laid out by the landscape artist Marty Poirier as an extension of the library environment. Within the high enclosing wall, which provides security, readers may, on most days of the year, find places to read beneath the trees, and the trees to the south give extra shade to the building. Scented plants such jasmine and sage add a sensory dimension both to the garden and, when the windows are open, to the interior of the building.

In its architectural language the building reflects the Modernist type that flourished in Southern California in the mid-20th century. The repetitive steel frame calls to mind the 'Case Study' houses. This lineage is clearly revealed in the architects' exploded

↑
General view of the interior. This shows the clear differentiation and expression of structure and services.

↑
View of the main entrance from within the garden courtyard.

axonometric drawing that shows the building as three distinct tectonic systems located above the foundation plan: the structural system, the enclosure system and the mechanical system. These distinct systems are clearly expressed in the execution of the building, where the artificial light fittings and the air-conditioning ducts are seen suspended below the unadorned roof structure. All the other elements – bookcases, book-check desk, study carrels – stand in a coherent relationship within this ordered space.

Environmental quality
The result is an internal environment that captures and responds to the variations of temperature and light that occur outside. Only when those variations compromise comfort – when it is too hot or cold or too dark –

is it necessary to resort to mechanical services. For much of its life the building will gently moderate the Californian climate to sustain the life of the library in all its rich diversity. Visitors are invited to make their own contribution to this process by choosing where to work, in the sun or in the shade, inside the building or in the garden. They can open or close windows at will. It is predicted that the building will consume only about half the energy of a typical modern library elsewhere in San Diego.

In a state where energy consumption often exceeds supply, a building like this clearly indicates a solution to the crisis. It suggests that it is not necessary to abandon the Kyoto resolutions on the global environment in favour of ever-higher consumption of fossil fuels or to expand our reliance on nuclear energy.

Conclusion
At face value the Carmel Mountain Ranch library is a modest building. It occupies an unambiguous position in our taxonomy of environmental architecture, being emphatically 'selective' in its strategy and adopting a tectonic of 'exposed power'. It is clear-cut and lucid and, as such, is a good example of the successful collaboration between architect and environmental engineer. A reinterpretation of the spirit of the 'Case Study' houses, which played such an important part in adapting the original propositions of the Modern Movement to the culture and climate of Southern California, it illustrates that these principles continue to be relevant as a response to the more specific and urgent environmental agenda of the 21st century.

The over-sailing roof
creates a sheltered
outdoor reading
space.

Interior showing
study area with
individually openable
windows.

The Exclusive Mode

Helicon Building

Sheppard Robson
London, UK
1996

➜
The envelope of the
Helicon Building is an
integral part of the
environmental
system.

Modern developments in urban office design can be traced back to a seminal paper by Leslie Martin and Lionel March, 'Land Use and Built Forms'.[1] Published in 1966, it demonstrated that, on large urban sites, court forms, through their inherent geometrical properties, achieve more efficient land use than isolated pavilions, and that court forms offer environmental advantages, particularly in respect of daylighting. A later study by Dean Hawkes and Richard MacCormac,

published in 1978, examined the environmental and energy-demand implications of glazing over the central courtyards of urban buildings.[2] This showed that such forms could, if carefully designed, achieve significant energy savings, up to 50 per cent, compared with typical air-conditioned buildings of that date.

The Helicon office project draws on these classic studies in that it involves the specific environmental and energy concerns embraced by the notion of

'sustainability'. The studies investigated a transformation of the urban courtyard form in which the central space has the potential to become a 'sustainable island' within the established urban fabric. Designed in the early 1990s, the Helicon project continues this line of thought by proposing a way in which the existing unsustainable city might be progressively transformed through adaptive design. For example, the layered wall conceived as a protective

147

The double skin
façade is punctuated
by service cores.

Transparency is a
theme for the whole
building.

and adaptable skin designed to lessen the energy load is carefully integrated with the environmental system.

In the early 1990s the retailer Marks & Spencer opened a takeaway food store in Moorgate, London. The store was so successful that it struggled to cope with demand and facilities on the site were found wanting. In particular, unloading facilities were inadequate to cope with store turnover and articulated trucks were forced to drive around the narrow city streets waiting for gaps in the loading and unloading sequence. The city block on the other side of Moorgate bounded by Finsbury Pavement, South Place, Dominion Street and Lackington Street had been acquired by London and Manchester Assurance in the recession of the early 1990s. Although at the time the acquisition may have appeared unpromising,

Marks & Spencer, who were prepared to take a 125-year lease, and another potential anchor tenant, Midland Bank, suggested that the development of the site might be commercially viable. The developer decided to combine offices with retail, and the eventual achievement of almost 50 per cent potential pre-let space allowed a start to be made on the development of the Helicon.

Site and climate
The building occupies a full city block in London's financial district. Bounded by busy city streets on all four sides, the block is virtually an island. Office developments in the heart of cities – where high levels of atmospheric pollution, noise and unwanted solar gain combine to make an unattractive cocktail – are generally confined to hermetically sealed boxes that can

keep out the worst of the city's environmental effects.

Form
Recent city building design has been typified by bland, blind boxes or overblown exercises in 'look-at-me' architecture. In the few developments where contextual design has been on the agenda, the result has been confused and confusing stylistic gestures. The Helicon combines retail accommodation, offices and a bank, which gave the designers the opportunity not only to respond to the complexity of the site's former uses but also to tackle the issue of the deep-plan high-energy city-office building. Six floors of speculatively developed office floors sit on top of three floors of retail. The six floors wrap around the ubiquitous atrium, but in this case the floors are terraced

Section of the Helicon Building.
The third to eighth floors contain
lettable office space.

Ground, third and
seventh levels.

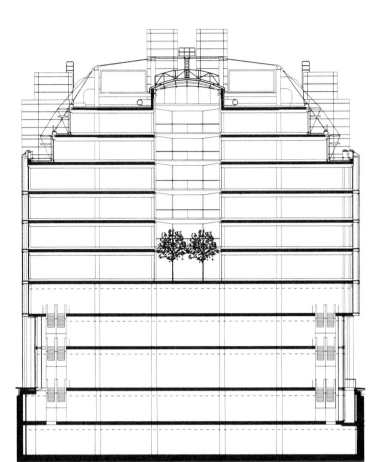

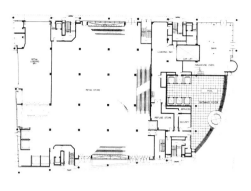

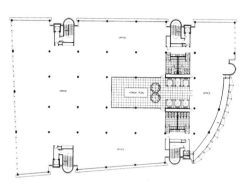

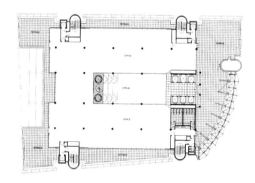

in the manner of a vineyard. Upper floors are set back like attic storeys from the pavement edge to diminish the overall bulk of the building mass. Punctuating the block is a stair and lift tower; these elements are 'inset' so that they appear to be 'outboard' of the main floor plates in the manner of the Lloyds Building. Graham Anthony of Sheppard Robson had been responsible for the design of the services towers for Richard Rogers in the Lloyds Building, and the same clear articulation, if not total separation, of served and servant spaces is also evident at the Helicon.

The stairs are bull-nosed and the lifts are rectangular. Their twin shafts are clad in silver metal panels (also reminiscent of Lloyds), making solid elements that provide a counterpoint to the glazed transparent elements of the remainder of the building

envelope. The main entrance to the offices is signalled by a curved suspended glass screen over double-height doors on the corner of Moorgate. The quadrant-shaped entrance, with entry on the diagonal, is simply shifted back to the orthogonal grid so that the main core including toilets and lift shafts runs the entire width of the block at the head of the atrium.

Layout
The width and depth of the office floors vary from level to level, but the floor plates reflect a traditional modular approach to office planning. The floors are based on a 1.5m (5ft) planning grid to provide maximum flexibility for the wide-ranging needs of potential tenants. The width of the floor plate is generally 16.5m (54ft) – made up of 9m (30ft) and 7.5m (25ft)

structural bays – from external window to atrium window. Exceptions to this occur in the section of floor that steps with the atrium. At the widest point the floor is more than 20m (66ft), but this reduces to approximately 10m (33ft) for the top two office floors. The atrium is roofed with a glazed barrel vault and sits above the Marks & Spencer store linked to the double-height entrance by an all-glass lift core. The atrium consists of a 9m (30ft) wide slot scooped out of the middle of the building form. The floors are sealed to the atrium with clear glazing to optimize daylighting to this edge of the office floor.

Structure and construction
The structure consists of a post-tensioned *in-situ* concrete-floor structure supporting raised floor offices above headroom. Walls are

149

The double skin contains a 0.9m (3ft) void.

Blinds, housed within the double skin, are shown here in various modes. Blinds should only be down for some 20–30 per cent of the year.

fully glazed externally and internally. Solar-control glass, including tinted and reflective glass, was avoided to maximize the potential for daylighting. The external skin is single-glazed frameless glass, bolt-fixed in front of a 0.9m (3ft) wide void. The outer skin can be opened or closed at the top and the bottom in response to changing temperatures and wind conditions.

While the inner skin remains sealed, the outer skin acts as a buffer to noise and temperature. Inside the void, large horizontal louvres are fitted between skins. Like giant Venetian blinds, these may be raised or lowered, tilted or turned, depending on solar conditions. The louvres are carefully spaced to avoid visual obstruction and they are perforated so that some daylight penetration is possible even when they are fully

tilted. The gap between the two skins makes a 0.9m (3ft) void – wide enough to allow access for full maintenance of the external envelope. Detailing of the external envelope and the skin inside the atrium is crisp and spare, heightening the whole building's sense of transparency.

Energy and environment
The standard solution for providing comfortable and healthy office environments in dense urban contexts in the 1980s and 1990s was variable-air-valve air-conditioning. At Helicon the objective was to find a low-energy alternative which would integrate with the external envelope and overall form of the building.

The ventilated façade
While a fully glazed façade is useful in maximizing daylight penetration,

problems of solar gain and glare have to be solved in order to provide a comfortable visual environment and also to limit cooling loads. In the design of the Helicon, Sheppard Robson worked with Arup to maximize transparency of the envelope while including a low-energy heating and ventilation system. A range of commonly used techniques including tinted and mirrored types of glass and external sun-shading were considered, but all were found to have a number of disadvantages. None of the coated glasses met the need for transparency, while external sun-shading added to maintenance and cleaning difficulties. The best option proved to be the glazed double-skin façade.

The double skin is an environmental buffer that moderates the effects of

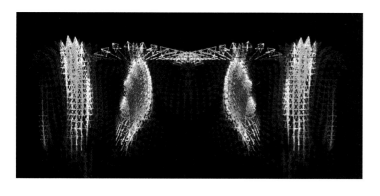
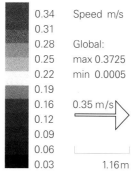

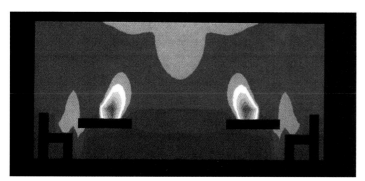
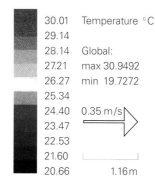

0.34	Speed m/s	
0.31		
0.28	Global:	
0.25	max 0.3725	
0.22	min 0.0005	
0.19		
0.16	0.35 m/s	
0.12		
0.09		
0.06		
0.03	1.16 m	

30.01	Temperature °C	
29.14		
28.14	Global:	
27.21	max 30.9492	
26.27	min 19.7272	
25.34		
24.40	0.35 m/s	
23.47		
22.53		
21.60		
20.66	1.16 m	

CDF studies of the office environment.

climate on the internal environment. When the air temperature is below 20°C (68°F), the void of the double skin is closed so that the whole wall can provide a warm layer of air next to the inner glazed wall. In summer the void is ventilated at the top and bottom. Acting as a thermal flue, a flow of air is created to promote a cooler layer of air. This is supplemented by carefully designed solar control.

Within the 0.9m (3ft) wide zone are perforated maintenance walkways and binds with 4.5m (15ft) wide perforated blinds that can be lowered and tilted. The mechanism for raising and lowering the blinds is automatically controlled by a solarimeter that measures the intensity of solar radiation and a light sensor on the façade. A light sensor and thermostat are positioned inside the offices to control the inclination of the louvre blades. The louvres on either side of each given floor are controlled as a group. A full-size mock-up of the system was made and tested by the design team in collaboration with Technical Blinds and carefully integrated with the design of the building services. The shading and ventilation of the void was predicted to reduce peak summertime solar gain by two-thirds, in turn reducing peak cooling requirements. The floor-to-ceiling glazing on both external and atrium skins optimizes potential for day-lighting across the office floor plate. Electric lighting is designed to supple-ment the daylighting and provide a general lighting level of 400 lux.

Chilled ceilings
Reductions in solar gain permitted the use of chilled ceilings to deal with the office cooling loads. This is fairly standard practice today, but in the early 1990s, when Helicon was in the design phase, the integration of an intelligent skin with this kind of system was a design innovation. In 1992 Arup made comparative studies of heating and ventilation systems, highlighting the fact that, while the combination of chilled ceilings and underfloor heating was not the lowest cost alternative, other benefits would accrue from this system. Although fan-coil units were about 15 per cent cheaper, plant space required by chilled ceilings was about 50 per cent that of a conventional variable-air-volume system. Fan-coil units appeared to be higher maintenance than chilled ceilings, and the comparison also indicated that chilled ceilings could allow a 16 per cent saving in energy costs.

The ventilated façade means that solar gain is managed, despite maximizing glazing for daylight.

Delicate detailing of the envelope articulates the office entrance at the south-west corner.

As chilled beams were considered by the design team to be visually intrusive, other options for chilled ceilings were investigated. Arup was not keen to use chilled ceiling panels that had to be clipped to the ceiling tiles, but just at that time a system was launched that incorporated demountable perforated metal ceiling tiles concealing flattened copper tubes with braided steel flexible connections to the chilled water supply. This is the system adopted in the building.

Air is supplied at 18°C (64°F) from under the floor at $2.5l/s/m^2$ $(0.0082ft^3/s/ft)$ – approximately three air changes per hour– while the flow temperature to the chilled ceiling is 15°C (59°F). Computational flow design studies showed that the combination was enough to maintain the temperature at a summer maximum of 23°C (73°F), while the radiant effect of the ceiling would make the space more comfortable.

Plant and distribution

Although it would have been possible to tap into the heating and cooling network of the City of London – allowing what would have otherwise been plant-room space to be replaced by office space – this appeared to have little economic benefit, and the need for reliability persuaded the design team to opt for on-site plant. Chillers, boilers, switch rooms and tank rooms are located in the basement, while the landlord's generator, air-handling units and cooling towers are at roof level. Four vertical cores distribute services to the floors, and air is ducted from the risers to the pressurized floor plenum. The system demands that the building skin is tight and a strict leakage specification of $0.35l/sm^2$ $(0.0011ft^3/s/ft^2)$ at 50 Pa was set. Extract is via a similar plenum at high level as exhaust air through the luminaries. Air supplied is not 100 per cent fresh; up to 40 per cent is recirculated depending on the enthalpy of the outside air.

Conclusion

Helicon represents a milestone in the development of the sustainable urban office. The combination of intelligent skin and covered atrium allows the installation of efficient low-energy servicing systems and improved comfort for office workers. This marks a step function change in the design of the office building and represents a new stage towards the development of urban offices as producers, rather than consumers, of energy.

Villa VPRO Offices
MVRDV
Rotterdam, Netherlands
1997

→
Villa VPRO's façade at
night, revealing the
dynamic of the
building interior.

The design of the workplace, particularly of the late 20th-century office, has been virtually reduced to a system based on 'shell, core and fit out'. Efficient in its use of space and with built-in ease of construction and servicing, the system is loved equally by developers and facilities managers – but all too often the result is neutral space that can be occupied by anyone but belongs to no one. Individuality is crushed and privacy is eroded. As Peter Davey has commented, 'the acres of hot-desking are as spiritually uplifting as a visit to the Gobi Desert, where grey sand is blown in your teeth and stuffs your nose'.[1]

Have architects done anything to improve the workplace? Only one or two examples spring to mind, among them Centraal Beheer at Apeldoorn by Herman Hertzberger (1973), where spaces in which individuals can work in isolation or as part of a community are arranged around communal pedestrian streets. The Dutch architectural tradition attaches more importance to real life than to theory. As might be expected, therefore, when a young firm of Dutch architects was commissioned to design a new workplace for a Dutch broadcaster, the traditional 'shell, core and fit out' system was not top of the agenda.

VPRO is an independent broadcasting company based in Hilversum which enjoys a reputation for high-quality television and radio programmes and is funded by voluntary subscriptions. Its popularity – reflected in increasing subscriber numbers – led VPRO in 1993 to decide to move to a purpose-built headquarters on a greenfield site in the grounds of the National Broadcasting Centre in Hilversum. The company originally operated from villa-type properties that, as a result of expansion, had become scattered across the city, with staff increasingly working in a variety of rooms, ranging from first-floor

↑

Site plan showing the 56m by 56m (184ft by 184ft) building amongst its neighbours.

piani nobili to attics and sun lounges. The villas had played a vital role in establishing VPRO's identity.

Having decided to rationalize operations in a single building on a campus shared with other television and broadcasting companies, VPRO wondered how it could preserve its accustomed workplace informality in a modern office building. The brief was that the new building should evoke the spirit and atmosphere of the villas without replicating them, and allow informal and vital connections between people inside and outside the organization to be re-created. The main activities at VPRO are programme research and design, radio broadcasting, programme editing, central archiving and customer services. Through research by MVRDV and extensive discussion with the company and individual staff,

the original standard headquarters building brief was revised, and the concept of the 'big villa' emerged from a holistic approach.

Site and context
The idea of the 'big villa' was compromised by a number of site constraints. Zoning and height restrictions meant that the building had to be developed in very compact form. The result is a five-storey building, 9,000m² (96,840ft²) in area with a footprint of 56m by 56m (184ft by 184ft) – thought to be the deepest office plan in the Netherlands. It is hard to determine the relationship between the new VPRO building and the surrounding villas. The site constraints and strict building codes forced MVRDV to develop informal and intimate interconnecting spaces by subtracting from the deep plan,

rather than by the more obvious step of additive pavilion-type structures. The building is partly recessed into its hilly site to stay within height restrictions.

Building form and organization
Differences between the inside and outside of the building have been blurred by what is called 'precision bombing', which has produced a number of deep shafts and slits in the plan, enabling spaces to flow into each other and connect.[2] The distinction between different levels is also unusual in that the conventional orthogonal floor plates are stepped and ramped. The building is entered at first-floor level via a sloping landscaped car park that continues as the first-floor slab into the building and then folds back on itself to form the second floor. These folding floor

158

↓
Sections of the
building: south–north
(top) and east–west.

→
Floor plans: (from
bottom to top, left
to right) basement;
ground; second;
third; fourth; and
fifth.

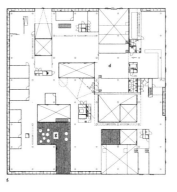
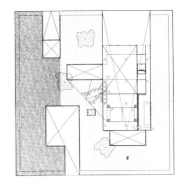
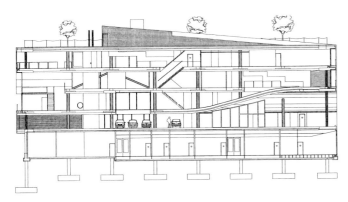
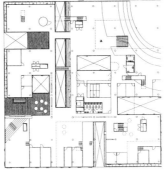
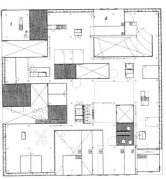
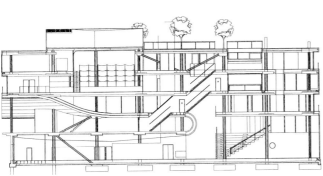

plates form a relatively continuous interior space incorporating hills, ramps, stairs and small faults negotiated by small flights of steps, offering as wide (if not wider) a range of spaces as that enjoyed in the original villas.

The car park runs under the porch framed by the canopy of the folded slab, and the main entrance to the building is through a glass box that sits in the car park occupying most of the plan at that level. The entrance 'is neither welcoming nor even immediately obvious. It's just that there can be nowhere else to go.'[3] From here visitors have to negotiate either Dutch 'stepladder' stairs or lift to reach the double-height reception area.

Structure and materials
Arup's VPRO structure is principally a reinforced-concrete floor slab supported on an orthogonal grid of circular columns. The grid is 7.5m by 7.5m (25ft by 25ft); while this integrates with the car park, the wide variety of workspaces is not determined by a regular planning grid. The system was chosen because it offered maximum flexibility in terms of the deformation and stopping of floor plates and the creation of voids. The fact that the two-way spanning slab could be cantilevered, cut, slotted and folded without using beam elements was put to maximum use. The floor-slab profile is expressed externally and the twists, turns and steps in the building can be read on all four elevations. Beams were confined to spaces such as the stepping restaurant. The vertical part of the folded plate acts as a beam as well as a wall in this condition. Steel cruciform shear heads are embedded

in the slabs at each column/floor junction and column up-stand shear heads are also used to enable slab thickness to be minimized. As well as limiting overall floor-to-floor heights, the spatial compression of the folded slab is accentuated. Columns are not permitted through voids. In the situation where the void is a double-grid width the two deep-transfer beams are employed at roof level and these become part of the urban landscape at this level.

The building form at Villa VPRO eliminated the traditional cores and the structural stability they provide in skeletal office buildings, so stability was added through the development of structural steel tube stability braces; these appear to be distributed randomly around the building but they transfer wind loads from one floor to the next. The floor plate then

159

↑ →

Floor plates are cut-peeled and even rolled away, in order to pierce and manipulate what would otherwise be a very deep plan.

distributes these forces to the next layer of braces on the level below. Such a system provides a high degree of flexibility when it comes to where to position bracing; visible bracing is placed around floor plates in order to open or close vistas, or to create visual elements that are severe or dynamic and dissonant.

To enable the structural topography to be expressed externally, façades are almost entirely glazed. Thirty-five types and colours of glass are used to deal with solar gain and thermal performance. Each particular type of glass is matched to its place and orientation, and supplemented with fixed and dynamic shading, balcony overhangs, blinds and plants. The result is a vivid geometry (especially when seen at night) that creates an exciting mosaic matching the dynamic of the building's interior.

Environment and services
Villa VPRO meets the Dutch regulations for office spaces regarding natural lighting and the requirement for all work stations to be within 5m (16ft) of a view. The building mass is cut, slotted, scooped and 'kebab'd' to provide slots for air and light. Nearly every office has access though a door to a patio, garden, terrace or balcony, and the distinction between inside and outside is constantly subdued even in the middle of the building. The primary aim of providing a wide variety of spatial settings for work is met by these formal moves but this strategy sets new challenges for the environmental designer.

Studies using both physical and computational models were carried out by Arup and DGMR to establish daylight conditions, façade heat gains

and losses, internal and external shading, and acoustics. These studies were part of an interactive process and helped to establish the final form, position and geometry of voids. Arup adopted a number of servicing approaches to support the multitude of different spaces and workplace configurations, and at the same time to minimize the visual impact of services. Given that the folded concrete slab leading people through the interior was a key concept of the design, it was not an option to adopt the conventional discreet distribution of services through suspended ceilings. Exposed concrete surfaces to floor and ceilings could not be cluttered with service ducts. Maximum use was therefore made of natural ventilation in spaces close to the envelope edge.

In most parts of the plan a raised floor plenum delivers conditioned air

← ↑
A wide range of
working contexts and
environments are
available for the
building users.

to the spaces, while in areas such as the restaurants and studio dedicated air-handling units deal with the higher loads demanded by increased ventilation rates. Editing suites incorporate chilled beams to complement the optimized fresh air delivered from the main air-handling units. The pedestal-type raised floor has a solid screed finish, and the void was used for power and communications distribution as well as a plenum.

The irregular floor plates, each with their particular and peculiar floor voids, present challenges for the integration of services. Discontinuity and remote spaces were a special problem. The building is designed with six principal risers carefully situated to deliver services to all areas of the building. Service runs are therefore minimized and the floor void

is optimized. The complexity of form over the deep plan means that the challenge of service rationalization and distribution is extended to the design of drainage above ground.

Conclusion
In the work of MVDRV the demands of programme, once defined, are cast in stone through their method of 'systematic realization'.[4] These programmatic constraints and the strict Dutch regulations have been applied to the letter at Villa VPRO to generate a bewildering variety of spaces. In the hands of an engineer and environmental designer not in tune with each space, this complex situation could result in chaos. At VPRO the system of 'shell, core and fit out' has not been abandoned entirely but intelligently modified to accommodate the spatial complexity

while providing an appropriate system of structural and environmental support. Villa VPRO may be regarded as characteristic of the architecture of the emerging global age and christened by some as 'Supermodernism'.[5] In the Dutch tradition of the nondescript box with a spatially complex inner world, the building challenges preconceived ideas about the workplace but is not as cold and scenographic as, say, the work of Rem Koolhaas.

← The roof is an integral part of the promenade.

↑ Façade detail showing how the building form has been manipulated to ensure inhabitants have access to daylight and views.

Beyeler Foundation Museum

Renzo Piano
Riehen, Basel
Switzerland
1997

The first art galleries were private affairs. Pictures collected by wealthy men were displayed in private salons for personal pleasure and enjoyment and to impress a close circle of friends and acquaintances. The first buildings providing public access often resembled what Tom Markus has described as 'a safe well-lit warehouse'.[1] Since then the art gallery has evolved, often to meet the environmental conditions demanded by the conservation of fragile but valuable artefacts. The gallery has incrementally been reduced to more of a safe warehouse and the designer's role is now often confined

to exercises in formal excess in order to signify that here lies culture accompanied by some new image of civitas. To challenge the technical migration of the gallery towards the scenographic and exclusive mode of environmental control and head back towards a selective functional tradition requires the marriage of a particular client with a particular collection and a design team with the technical wherewithal.

The Beyeler Foundation Museum was designed and constructed to house the private collection of modern art belonging to Ernst Beyeler. The collection was built up

over a long period and consists of about 180 paintings, ranging from works by Monet to recent East German art. It includes works by Cézanne, Matisse, Picasso, Klee, Kandinsky, Rauschenberg and Lichtenstein, as well as sculptures by Giacometti and pieces from Easter Island and Oceania. International awareness of the collection was sparked by exhibitions in Madrid's Centro Reina Sofia, and a purpose-built gallery in Switzerland to house the collection was proposed. Ernst Beyeler wanted a naturally lit environment of calm and repose. In 1981 Dominique de Menil had

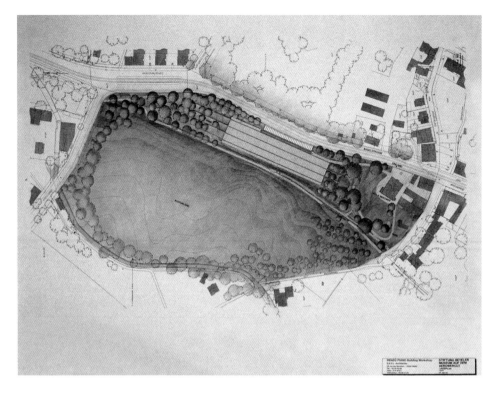

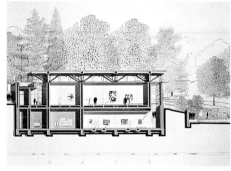

↑
Site plan: the gallery
runs parallel to the
north–south road.

↑
Aerial photography
and sectional model
show buffering and
containment of site.

entrusted Renzo Piano with the design of a new museum in Houston for the Menil Collection (see pages 174–181), one of the most important corpuses of surrealist and primitive African art. The idea was to create a non-monumental space open to contact with nature, facilitating a direct and relaxed relationship between visitor and artefact. Piano's solution – based on the design of daylit spaces under a sheltering roof that filtered the sky – was the inspiration for Beyeler. Impressed by the tranquil spaces of the Menil and determined to display his collection in natural light wherever possible, Beyeler asked his design team to create a protective lightweight canopy for the galleries which would modulate the effects of the sky and hover over the walls that the art is exhibited on.

Site

Riehen is an affluent suburb of Basel near the German border. The museum site is in parklike grounds that extend northwards along a road leading from the 18th-century Villa Berower. The entrance to both is marked by gates that stand opposite a tram terminus. Once inside the gates, visitors may enter the villa, which now houses the museum bookshop, cafeteria and offices, or walk on to the museum.

The new museum is designed as a pavilion running 120m (395ft) south–north from the villa and parallel to the road. The narrow rectangular plan is contained between a new boundary wall to the road and an existing stone retaining wall that runs alongside a path on the eastern edge of the park. The building offers a calm haven in which to study art and enjoy the views of the countryside to the west.

Form and layout

The form of the gallery is determined by long parallel walls running north–south which are expressed externally but disintegrate and break down internally. The 7.5m (25ft) wide space between the walls accommodates gallery spaces. Entry through the existing garden is along a path between boundary walls on the southern edge of the building. Here the ends of the 700mm (27½in) wide parallel walls are expressed below a great oversailing roof as they run beyond glazed openings to the galleries. This striated layering has been described as providing a 'view inwards...like an X-ray, cutting through this southerly elevation deep into the gallery space and the precious works of art'.[2] An angled boundary on the northern side of the building channels visitors towards the

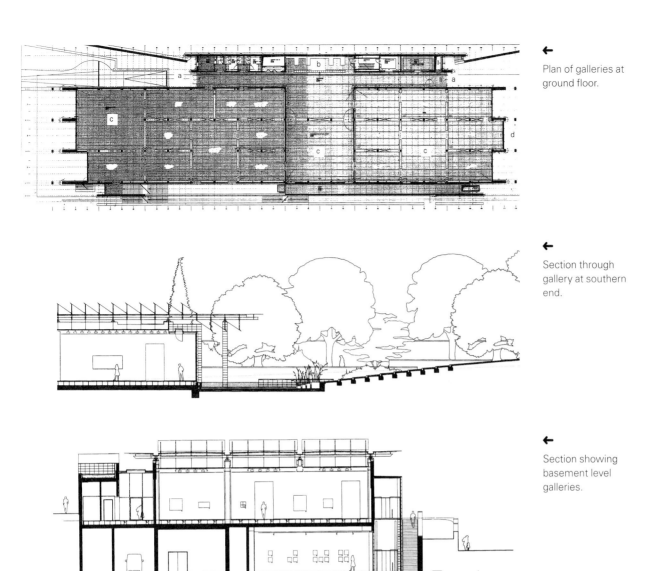

←

Plan of galleries at ground floor.

←

Section through gallery at southern end.

←

Section showing basement level galleries.

entrance. On this side there is a secondary set of doors and a vehicular ramp that leads to the basement storey, which provides accommodation for staff car parking, loading, storage space, workshops, plant rooms and an artificially lit gallery for light-sensitive works.

The lightweight oversailing roof canopy contrasts with the apparent heavyweight archaic walls, emphasizing the distinction between 'tectonic' and 'stereotomic' elements. The walls are interrupted and broken in order to provide a range of gallery spaces, typically 12m by 7.2m (39ft by 24ft) punctuated with larger exhibition spaces of 7.2m by 18m (24ft by 59ft) and 15.1m by 18m (50ft by 59ft).

Structure and construction

The lineal pavilion is constructed over a 4.3m (14ft) deep reinforced-concrete basement. The walls of the galleries are not structural but they contain reinforced-concrete columns at 6m (20ft) centres to support the roof. Roof overhangs are supported by steel columns also encased in stone. The four long walls, spaced at 7.8m (26ft) centres, each 108m (354ft) long and 6.1m (20ft) high, sit under a lightweight crystalline roof canopy 28.3m by 127m (93ft by 417ft) on plan.

The steel roof structure gives continuous support for the various glass layers, comprising glass ceiling and internal louvres, double-glazing, and the posts that carry the external inclined glass shading. Primary beams span continuously from east to west, while the secondary beams are arranged in pairs on either side of the columns, spanning 6m (20ft) in the north–south direction. Additional primary beams spanning north–south

on the main column lines create longer exhibition spaces. The 250mm (10in) deep beams, formed from steel plates, are carefully detailed. Primary beams have a box section with the flanges projecting outside the webs, so that their appearance is similar to that of the fabricated 'I' sections used for the secondary beams. The beam and column connections are also carefully configured. Using steel castings and bolts, the continuity of construction is broken on the centre line of the column. Forces and moments are transferred from inside to outside structural elements but cold-bridging is eliminated by the physical separation of the elements.

The complex roof construction is completed by white glass *brise-soleil*, supported on vertical steel tubular posts bolted to the top of beams on site with steel castings. Steel castings

←

The approach to the building from the south, exposing the clear tectonic of the structure.

→

Looking south, out to the lily pond.

are also used at the top of the posts to fix the *brise-soleil*. These top-bolted connections allow glass to slide parallel to glass, but also to take wind loads perpendicular to the glass so that differential deflections of the beams supporting the top and bottom of the plane of glass do not induce high stresses into it. The structure was designed to Swiss building codes to accommodate relatively high snow loading; as the building also lies within a seismic zone, horizontal forces are limited to around 7 per cent of the total vertical loads.

Visual environment

Ernst Beyeler had seen the Menil building in Houston designed by Piano and Arup and was committed to securing the same qualities of daylight in his museum as those at the Menil. It was agreed that daylight should be used as the light source across the whole ground floor, and that the design of the building should seek to maximize the number of hours during which the collection could be viewed by daylight. However, best-practice standards for exposure of works of art to daylight in terms of time, levels and spectral content could not be compromised by the desire to provide a daylit environment.

Following studies of lighting conditions in Basel, Arup recommended a target daylight factor of 4 per cent, which is around double that in most European galleries. An active shading system to control internal light levels within predetermined limits, particularly on bright summer days, was also prescribed as an essential part of the lighting strategy. These performance requirements were met by the development of a universal multi-layered roof. The outermost element is the layer of fitted glass brise-soleil inclined and positioned to prevent direct sun penetration during all museum opening times but also to maintain optimum admittance of diffused light. Below this lies the weatherproof layer consisting of a double-glazed skin with an ultraviolet filter that removes those parts of the electromagnetic spectrum most likely to damage the paintings to be displayed on the ground floor of the museum. Immediately below this layer are computer-motorized aluminium louvre blades that control light levels in each room of the museum. These levels can be arranged to suit the management of the building and the conservation of the collection. When the museum is closed, for example, the louvres are

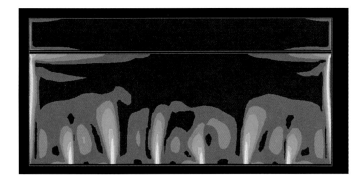

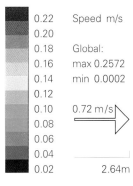

CFD study of displacement systems.

Air is delivered at low velocity through carefully integrated floor grilles.

closed to prevent exposure of artworks to daylight.

The louvre system lies in the zone between ceiling and roof, which is designed as a 'loft thermal buffer zone'[3] and combines with the external *brise-soleil* to prevent 98 per cent of incident solar radiation from reaching the gallery spaces below. The lower boundary of the loft is formed by a laminated-glass ceiling designed to support maintenance access to the louvre-blind motors and electric illumination in the loft. The electric illumination is designed to complement the daylighting strategy: as daylight fades, triphosphor linear fluorescent fittings gradually compensate for the loss, contributing to the maintenance of ideal lighting levels. The lowest layer in the system forms the visible ceiling of the ground-floor galleries: a grid of perforated-metal panels incorporates a paper that diffuses light once more and adds a layer of opacity to the contents of the 'loft thermal buffer zone'. The uniform lighting system is augmented by small low-voltage spotlights positioned on stems at the junctions of each ceiling panel. These can add high-lighting and directional light essential for modelling effects of sculpture.

Energy and environment

Thermal buffer spaces extend from the roof to the east and west sides of the façade, helping to limit the effects of climatic extremes on the building (-11°C (12°F) in winter, 33°C (91°F) in summer). The heated and ventilated loft means that, despite the 100 per cent glazed roof, perimeter heating is needed only in the north and southernmost galleries. The east façade is climatically buffered by the service and ancillary rooms, and to the west the 'winter garden' performs the same task, as well as providing a resting place with views across the countryside.

These buffer zones help to reduce reliance on mechanical systems – particularly important in Switzerland, where air conditioning is strongly discouraged in line with the national policy to abandon development of nuclear power and to reduce the country's reliance on predominantly nuclear-generated power from France. Regulatory frameworks therefore focus on the reduction of energy demand. In the case of this particular building type, a 'statement of need' must be submitted to the local authority that justifies the requirement for mechanical systems. The case for the Beyeler – based on the intention to display, conserve and

store valuable works of art – was supplemented by a dynamic analysis of annual energy use, as required by the local authority.

Heating and ventilation system

A true displacement system of ventilation was chosen for the Beyeler. This was designed to minimize air velocities in proximity to artwork. The air is delivered at very low velocities from linear floor grilles, which are made from wood to integrate both visually and functionally with the oak strip floor. Floorboards on either side of the grills can be removed to enable access to the ductwork plenum below (for cleaning) and to electrical sockets (for flexible display). Heating is limited to perimeter heating through trench connectors installed below the same wooden grilles under perimeter windows. The air supply to each

gallery module is controlled by variable-air-volume boxes installed in the services corridor at basement level. This 1.8m (6ft) wide space runs for most of the building length and contains supply and extract ducts, which are fed by two air-handling units, each able to provide up to 50 per cent fresh air in favourable external conditions. Additionally, the primary air-handling units each incorporate thermal wheels to recover heat from exhaust air in winter and also obtain further heat following dehumidification by transferring heat from the extract air.

Energy analysis

Using their own computer model, 'Energy 2', Arup carried out energy analysis. This model makes use of the thermal and radiation algorithm of the program 'Room' to analyze

dynamically the major spaces of the museum. Energy required by the building was calculated for every hour of the year based on real weather data from Basel.

The glass roof

The glass roof consists of approximately 4,000m^2 (43,060ft^2) of conventionally supported, double-glazed insulating units. As structural glazed roofs have become more in demand, codes of practice and design guidelines have been developed, but at Beyeler the roof included elements not covered by design guidance. In particular, the cantilevered glazed overhangs at the edge of the roof canopy presented a new challenge. The overhangs are outside the envelope of the building volume and therefore do not need to be double-glazed insulating units.

Laminated single-glazed panels were chosen, but the design of the four cantilevering corner panels required special attention. These panels are subject to loading conditions not covered by any codes because of their unique asymmetric configuration. Glass has a low tensile strength (compared with steel and reinforced concrete), which cannot be appreciably increased by variations in chemical composition. However, glass can effectively be pre-stressed by heat-treating; this produces different levels of residual compressive stress, which must be overcome before tensile failure can occur.

The corner panels therefore comprise a single pane 3.2m by 2.4m (10ft by 8ft) of heat-strengthened glass 8mm ($\frac{1}{3}$in) thick laminated on top of a 12mm ($\frac{1}{2}$in) thick toughened glass pane using four layers of 0.38mm

($\frac{1}{100}$in) thick polyvinyl butryl. The single pane is supported 0.9m (3ft) in from the short edge and 1.2m (4ft) in from the long edge, creating a 1.5m (5ft) cantilever to the free corner. If the toughened layer were placed on top in the conventional manner and were to break, collapse would be possible. Therefore, in this case, by placing the strengthened glass on top and employing the building layer if the toughened glass fractures, collapse is prevented as the upper layer works compositely with the broken layer.

Conclusion
Ernst Beyeler's collection had originally been installed in his home, where the works were daylit and came alive in naturally changing conditions. He wanted to re-create these conditions in the new gallery, and his desire has been largely fulfilled by

means of the distillation of architecture and engineering in the art of the environment. The spaces for display are tranquil and undisturbed by the intrusive visual noise of engineering and constructional technique.

Byzantine Fresco Chapel Museum

François de Menil
Houston, Texas
USA, 1997

➜
The concrete-clad
exterior from the
garden court.

The Menil Foundation in Houston has a distinguished record as a patron of the fine arts and of the work of contemporary architects. It has twice commissioned buildings from Renzo Piano: the Menil Collection museum, completed in 1986,[1] and the Cy Twombly Gallery, completed in 1995.[2] In 1990 it asked François de Menil to design a chapel museum to house two important Byzantine frescoes that had been stolen, during the late 1970s, from a small chapel at Lysi in Cyprus. Following their recovery and restoration, the frescoes were acquired by the Menil Foundation and returned to the Church of Cyprus, which handed them back to the foundation to be kept in safe custody on extended loan.

The frescoes, depicting Christ and the Virgin Mary, were taken from the dome and apse of the original chapel. In their restored form they are supported on back-up shells designed with the help of Peter Rice at Arup.[3] They are installed in the new building as two geometrical figures, of hemisphere and demi-hemisphere, dome and apse.

François de Menil's intention was to create a building that was simultaneously a museum and a

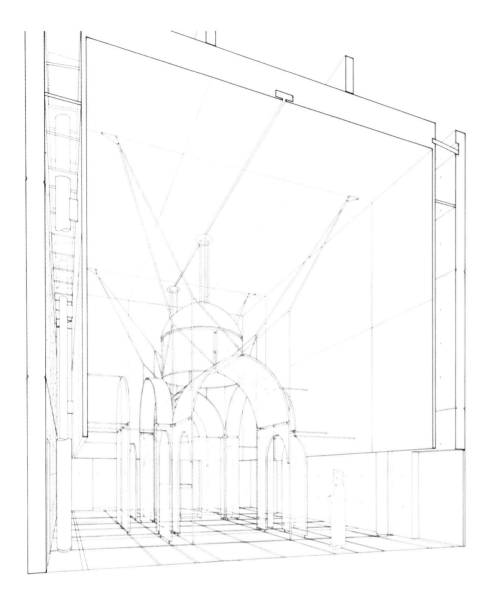

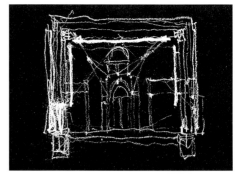

←

The sectional perspective reveals the cross-sectional hierarchy of the concrete enclosure, the secondary steel lining and the skeletal steel and glass of the chapel.

↑

An early sketch by François de Menil.

↑

The Byzantine chapel at Lysi, Cyprus, where the frescoes were originally painted.

consecrated Greek Orthodox chapel. The solution is a layered composition in which a skeletal 'reliquary box', which evokes the form of the historic chapel in Cyprus, is placed within a massive enclosing structure. The development of the design is a vivid demonstration of intensive collaboration between architect and engineer. Arup undertook all aspects of the engineering design.

Quantity and quality

It is a paradox that, in their dislocation from their original setting in a historic chapel, the frescoes have become subject to a set of environmental requirements that could not possibly have been met there. The technical brief demanded that, in their new home, they must be kept in an environment that met the most stringent curatorial standards for an art museum, including precise control of temperature, humidity, air quality and illumination exposure, but an overriding aim was to make a place in which the frescoes would resume their original status as objects of contemplation – to address the technical needs in a manner that, however elaborate the engineering, would sustain respect for the sacred.

Layers of environmental space

The site in the suburbs of Houston is enclosed by a rough-hewn perimeter wall of limestone, a reference to the materiality of the chapel in Cyprus. Within this, the box-like volume of the chapel has been constructed from load-bearing *in-situ* concrete, clad with precisely formed and finished precast concrete panels. The space is 9.1m (30ft) wide, 14m (46ft) long and 8.8m (29ft) high. Smaller concrete and lead-clad volumes, containing ancillary spaces, including the sacristy, cluster around this. Entrance is through a narthex-like space that slips between the perimeter wall and the chapel enclosure.

The strategy of layering continues in the interior, where a steel-framed structure supports a further enclosure of dark, sheet-steel walls and the roof slab. This internal volume is suspended from eight tubular steel columns and terminates 2.4m (8ft) above the floor. It is separated from the concrete box by a 600mm (23½in) wide toplit space. Within this, the form of the chapel is delineated by a delicate and precise framework of steel tubes which, in their turn, carry panels and arches of 38mm (1½in) thick laminated, annealed, white water glass. In a precise recreation of the form and dimensions of the original building, the frescoes of dome and

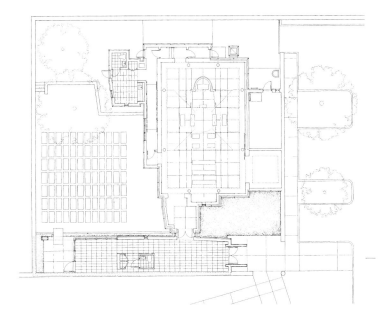

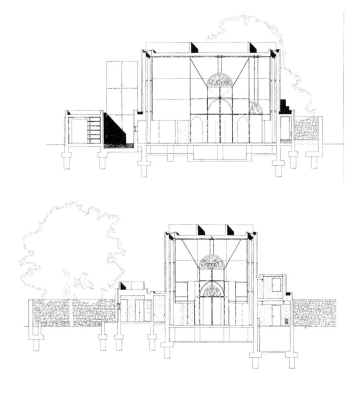

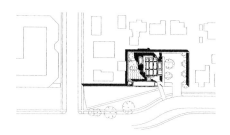

↑
The plan of the
building shows the
chapel within the
perimeter enclosure
of the courtyard.

→
The cross-sections
show how the glass
chapel is enclosed and
sustained by the
surrounding
structures. The
underfloor plenum
space plays an

essential role in the
environmental
strategy of the
building.

apse float in their new space. The overlapping of the external and internal enclosures ensures that direct daylight and sunlight are excluded from the centre of the space. Natural light cascades down the finely finished grey concrete and is reflected upwards by a perimeter strip of limestone paving. Within the inner space all surfaces are dark – black-painted steel and a dark slate floor. These absorb the daylight and create the setting in which the fictional recreation of the chapel may establish its presence.

The chapel structure is a welded tubular-steel plane frame that, almost imperceptibly, supports the laminated glass elements that define its overall form. Concealed artificial light sources reflect and refract from and within the thick sheets of glass and the structure appears to float weightlessly in the

space. These gently glowing surfaces bathe the frescoes in an even and controlled light. Artificial light comes from two sources. First, an array of fluorescent lamps is positioned in narrow slots cut into the floor directly beneath each vertical glass panel to uplight them delicately. The second source is a series of small tungsten halogen luminaires attached to the steel structure. Wiring concealed within the structural frame carries the low voltage supply to these. At night fluorescent lighting between the steel and concrete enclosures replaces daylight and maintains the calculated balance of illumination.

Thermal control
Environmental layers are key to the thermal strategy of the design. The almost unpunctured, sealed envelope acts to exclude the heat of the

Houston summer and its thermal mass stabilizes the internal environment. The reflectant surface of the precast concrete cladding helps to reduce the transmittance of direct solar radiation. The process of exclusion is further supported by the function of the entrance and sacristy, which act as buffer zones and are air-conditioned independently by heat-pump units mounted on their rooftops. The chapel is positively pressurized further to reduce the infiltration of outside air.

The function of the building as a place of worship created the need to make an environment fit for human habitation. Computer models were used extensively in the design process to analyse thermal performance and to reduce the loads and operation of the mechanical plant. The chapel is air-conditioned as a

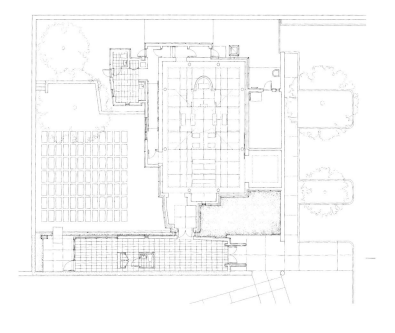

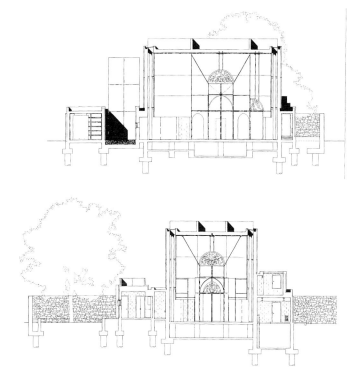

↑

The plan of the
building shows the
chapel within the
perimeter enclosure
of the courtyard.

→

The cross-sections
show how the glass
chapel is enclosed and
sustained by the
surrounding
structures. The
underfloor plenum
space plays an

essential role in the
environmental
strategy of the
building.

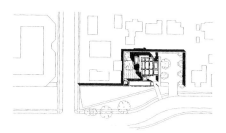

apse float in their new space. The
overlapping of the external and
internal enclosures ensures that direct
daylight and sunlight are excluded
from the centre of the space. Natural
light cascades down the finely
finished grey concrete and is reflected
upwards by a perimeter strip of
limestone paving. Within the inner
space all surfaces are dark – black-
painted steel and a dark slate floor.
These absorb the daylight and create
the setting in which the fictional
recreation of the chapel may establish
its presence.

The chapel structure is a welded
tubular-steel plane frame that, almost
imperceptibly, supports the laminated
glass elements that define its overall
form. Concealed artificial light sources
reflect and refract from and within the
thick sheets of glass and the structure
appears to float weightlessly in the

space. These gently glowing surfaces
bathe the frescoes in an even and
controlled light. Artificial light comes
from two sources. First, an array of
fluorescent lamps is positioned in
narrow slots cut into the floor directly
beneath each vertical glass panel to
uplight them delicately. The second
source is a series of small tungsten
halogen luminaires attached to the
steel structure. Wiring concealed
within the structural frame carries the
low voltage supply to these. At night
fluorescent lighting between the steel
and concrete enclosures replaces
daylight and maintains the calculated
balance of illumination.

Thermal control

Environmental layers are key to the
thermal strategy of the design. The
almost unpunctured, sealed envelope
acts to exclude the heat of the

Houston summer and its thermal
mass stabilizes the internal
environment. The reflectant surface of
the precast concrete cladding helps to
reduce the transmittance of direct
solar radiation. The process of
exclusion is further supported by the
function of the entrance and sacristy,
which act as buffer zones and are air-
conditioned independently by heat-
pump units mounted on their
rooftops. The chapel is positively
pressurized further to reduce the
infiltration of outside air.

The function of the building as a
place of worship created the need to
make an environment fit for human
habitation. Computer models were
used extensively in the design
process to analyse thermal
performance and to reduce the loads
and operation of the mechanical plant.
The chapel is air-conditioned as a

← The restored fresco as it 'floats' above its new enclosure.

↑ The fresco before restoration.

→ Detail of the softly illuminated glass structure.

single zone with a dedicated air-handling unit located in the basement, which delivers conditioned air to a sealed basement plenum below the chapel floor and, from there, into the space through a continuous grille at the perimeter, between the limestone and slate floors. This delivers air precisely to control the effects of any solar gains or heat losses that result from the perimeter rooflight directly above. A second series of inlets is positioned directly beneath the vertical glass panels, where they mark the outline of the enclosure in the floor. These inlets are also occupied by the concealed fluorescent lamps that light the panels, elegantly combining both systems.

The installation uses the principle of displacement air distribution within the chapel, which ensures that the conditions are uniform throughout the space, meeting the needs of both the frescoes and the human visitors. Extraction is through an opening in the ceiling above the frescoes, and the condition of the returned air is monitored to control the condition of the supply air. The system uses a relatively high air-change rate so that effective filtration of the supply can be achieved; this required thorough acoustic analysis and the design of noise-control measures to ensure that the plant is appropriately quiet. Before the frescoes were installed, the entire system was tested *in-situ*.

Conclusion

In comparison with most of the other works in this book, the chapel museum is a small and specialized building but, as we suggest above, its significance in this context lies in the fact that re-housing the frescoes demanded such precise and complex collaboration of architecture and engineering to ensure their survival.

In our modern culture we have assumed a new sense of responsibility for and custodianship of the past, so that such contrivance has become a necessity. In his essay *Travels in Hyperreality*, Umberto Eco proposed that this is a particularly American phenomenon, in which the authentic and the ersatz may be confused by the perfection with which they are executed. [4] But the demand for the long-term conservation of works of art is now universal and this small building in Houston stands as a demonstration of the capability of contemporary architectural and engineering practice to reconcile the needs of the qualitative and the quantitative.

In the completed building, the chapel is suspended in its layers of natural and artificial illumination.

Museum of Contemporary Art

Josef Paul Kleihues
Chicago, USA
1996

When Chicago's Museum of Contemporary Art was founded in 1967, it was housed in a building that a decade later was no longer able to meet the needs of either the growing permanent collection or the expanding programme of temporary exhibitions. In 1990 the site of the National Guard Armory building, on a well-preserved strip of parkland between Michigan Avenue and Lake Michigan, was chosen as the location for a new museum. One year later, the Berlin-based architect Josef Paul Kleihues was chosen to design the building, which was completed and opened to the public in 1996.

According to Andrea Mesecke and Thorsten Scheer, the authors of *Museum of Contemporary Art Chicago*, Kleihues, in formulating his approach, was influenced by 'a combination of European classicism, which of course was the origin of what was called rationalism in architecture since the late 1920s and something that is typical of Chicago...and the pragmatism that characterises Chicago's best architecture, its naked concentration on the task at hand'.[1]

In elaborating this analysis, Mesecke and Scheer referred explicitly to the work of the great 19th-century German classicist Karl Friedrich Schinkel.[2] Schinkel's designs for public buildings in Berlin, the Schauspielhaus (1818–21) and the Altes Museum (1822–28), provide strong authority for the representation of the cultural institution as an austere pavilion set axially in relation to a major public open space in the city. In addition, the Altes Museum serves as a powerful precedent for an art museum organized according to strict symmetrical principles. Both of these features are reflected in Kleihues's design for the Chicago museum.

The Chicago School of Architecture had its origins in the rapid

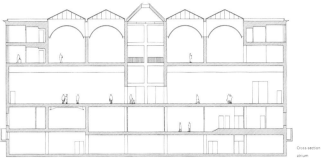

Cross-section
atrium

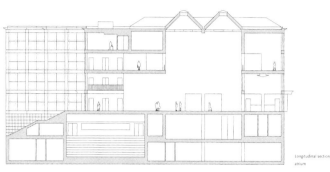

Longitudinal section
atrium

↑
The site plan showing
the Museum of
Contemporary Art in
a green canyon in the
central business
district of Chicago.

↑
The north–south
section (top) shows
the top-lit permanent
exhibition galleries
above the artificially-lit
spaces for temporary

exhibitions. In the
east–west section
(above) the spatial
significance of the
central atrium
is shown.

reconstruction and expansion of the city in the decades after 1871, when a fire destroyed much of the downtown area. During that period, architects such as William leBaron Jenney, H. H. Richardson, Burnham & Root, Holabird & Roche and Adler & Sullivan created a confident architectural language for the realization of the building programmes of the new metropolis.[3] In doing so, they rapidly assimilated and applied the developments in building technology that were taking place at the time. The result was an architecture that directly expressed its purpose and construction – the 'naked concentration of the task at hand' that was so admired by Kleihues. As regards the wider cultural background to the design for the Museum of Contemporary Art, it is worth noting that Chicago was the city in which

Mies van der Rohe settled in 1938, after his departure from Germany.

Site and programme
The site of the Museum of Contemporary Art has been described as a 'green canyon' within the dense urban fabric of Chicago's business district.[4] It is a 66.8m by 126.8m (219ft by 416ft) rectangle, with its long axis running east to west. To the west is the water tower and pumping station that has been a landmark in the city since the 19th century, and to the east an open park extends to the shores of Lake Michigan. Tall office blocks rise to the north and south.

The new building includes galleries for the museum's collection of contemporary art and for its rich programme of temporary exhibitions. There is also an outdoor sculpture garden, as well as the Mayer

Education Center, which incorporates a 300-seat auditorium, studio-classrooms and areas for live performances and symposia. Other amenities include a shop, a 15,000-volume art library and a café, as well as extensive storage and service spaces.

The design of a museum environment is governed by the need to maintain precise control over both the condition of the internal air and the illumination levels. In this case, the fact that Chicago suffers from severe atmospheric pollution – caused by gaseous and particulate pollutants carried into the city by the prevailing westerly winds – made particularly stringent demands on Arup's design of the mechanical services. From the start Kleihues was emphatic that the principal exhibition rooms should be naturally lit. He was

The permanent exhibition galleries achieve controlled daylighting through their layered system of translucent laylights, above which further control is provided by automatically operated louvres.

equally insistent that, rather than a 'cold', 'grey' northern light, there should be 'a wealth of light with all spectral colours'.

The classical tradition

Among the most apparent classical influences in the design of the museum are the symmetry of its plan and the adoption of the conventional horizontal organization into base, wall and cornice. The main entrance is reached by a sweeping flight of steps cut into a limestone-clad base reminiscent of Schinkel's Altes Museum. The entire building adheres to a geometrical order based on a repeated square of 7.8m by 7.8m (26ft by 26ft) and its subdivision into a secondary system of 3.9m (13ft). The overall plan of the building is contained within a seven by seven grid of these 7.8m (26ft) squares,

giving 54.6m (182ft), plus 0.3m (1ft) either side to allow for structural thickness – a total of 55.2m by 55.2m (184ft by 184ft). This geometrical discipline also applies to the cross-section. A module of 0.6m (2ft) is used to regulate all the minor dimensions and details of the building.

During the classical revival of the 19th century, complex environmental installations were incorporated into buildings. Eminent architects such as Adam, Soane, Barry and Elmes in England, Labrouste in France and Semper in Germany achieved a discreet synthesis of new technology and conventional architectural language. By declaring the influence of the European classical tradition, and in particular its revival in the 19th century, Kleihues implies a similar discretion in his environmental approach at the Chicago museum.

Structure and planning

The building consists of a reinforced-concrete structure based on the 7.8m (26ft) grid. At its heart is an atrium rising four storeys from first to fourth floors and topped by two truncated pyramidal rooflights, which establishes a sense of spatial continuity and orientation throughout the museum. The first-floor entrance on the west side of the building opens directly into a double-height vestibule that evokes the great entrance loggia of the Altes Museum. A broad passage leads ahead to the atrium and beyond to the double-height café, which overlooks the sculpture garden to the east. The temporary exhibition galleries are located on either side of the atrium.

As an alternative to the grand approach to the *piano nobile*, the building may be entered at ground

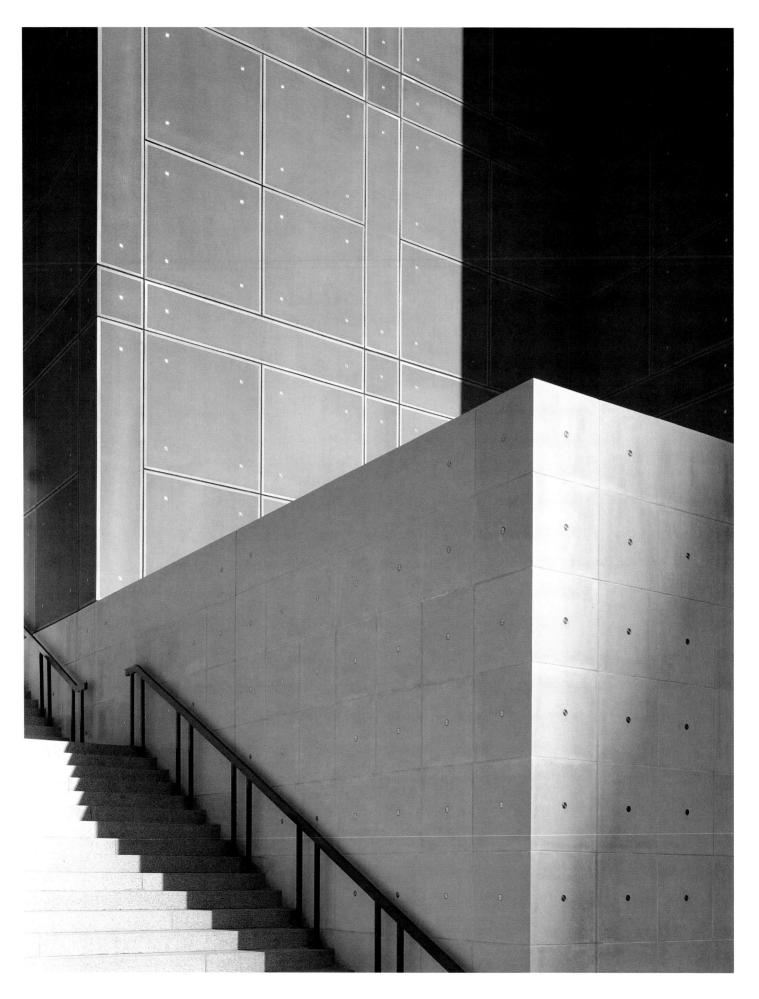

The stairs to the main entrance, cut into the limestone-clad base, above which rises the cast-aluminium cladding of the body of the building.

Looking up the steel and stone main staircase.

→

At the plinth level, in addition to the Meyer Education Center, the plan accommodates the principal service and plant rooms.

At the level of the main entrance, and of the temporary exhibition spaces, the dominant symmetry of the plan is established. The position of the four vertical service cores is clearly legible.

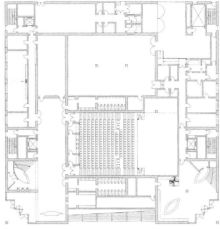

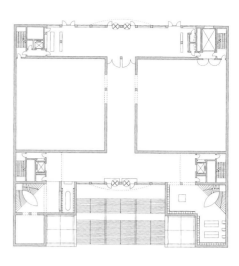

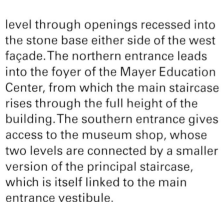

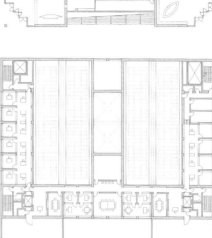

←

The permanent collection galleries are disposed either side of the central atrium at the upper level and the principal adminstrative offices occupy the attic spaces above the side galleries.

→

Looking west across the atrium at the upper level. The geometrical regulation of the entire building is expressed in the coordination of the grids of structure, fenestration and illuminated ceiling.

level through openings recessed into the stone base either side of the west façade. The northern entrance leads into the foyer of the Mayer Education Center, from which the main staircase rises through the full height of the building. The southern entrance gives access to the museum shop, whose two levels are connected by a smaller version of the principal staircase, which is itself linked to the main entrance vestibule.

On the fourth floor are the galleries for the permanent collection, which take the form of four rooflit, barrel-vaulted rooms placed two on either side of the atrium. Works that need protection from natural light are displayed in three small, artificially lit rooms opening off the southernmost gallery. The museum administration is located in a U-shaped mezzanine on the fifth floor.

The simple clarity and order of its materiality and detail reinforce the geometric logic of the building. Externally, above the limestone base, the structure is clad in cast-aluminium panels that delineate the underlying regulating dimensions. Window openings, where they occur, also conform to this order. Reminders of the geometry, evident throughout the interior, are most clearly identifiable in the atrium, in the pyramids of the rooflights and in the expressed structural frame. Elsewhere the gridded ceilings follow precisely the same system and organize the relationship of artificial light sources and outlets for the air-conditioning. The structural frame and walls are finished in unadorned white paint.

This quiet austerity is continued in the galleries for the permanent collection. Kleihues's desire to use

natural light as the principal light source in these rooms has led to a multi-layered roof construction in which translucent glass vaults are suspended beneath four continuous rooflights. A system of automatically controlled louvres in the ceiling void precisely regulates the light levels to which the pictures are exposed. Artificial lighting is integrated into this system. The temporary exhibition galleries on the lower floor are permanently artificially lit, providing the flexibility needed for the diverse exhibitions shown there.

Environmental response
The basis of the building's lighting design was the 'lux-hours' principle, which establishes maximum exposure levels for the various kinds of art work, defined as the product of light levels and hours of exposure per

annum. It proved necessary to prevent direct penetration of sunlight into the building. To ensure that exposure does not exceed the permitted levels, the illumination in the galleries is continuously monitored by photocells, which adjust the louvres above the ceiling vaults to reflect and filter the daylight without eliminating the full spectrum, in accordance with the architect's intentions. A filtering laminate incorporated in the external layer of the roof glazing excludes ultraviolet light, which is damaging to coloured pigments. The effect within the galleries of shadows cast by the surrounding tall buildings on the museum's glazed roof was reduced, but not eliminated, by using the adjustable louvre system.

Excluding atmospheric pollution was the greatest challenge in the design of the mechanical installations.

The Illinois Environmental Protection Agency confirmed that Chicago's atmosphere contained high levels of sulphur dioxide, nitrous oxides, ozone and chlorides, all of which are potentially damaging to works of art. The galleries are served by an air-handling unit that incorporates layers of filtration to eliminate particulate and chemical contaminants before the temperature and moisture content of the air is adjusted to the required levels. The system uses a network of sensors spread throughout the galleries to maintain the internal environment within the necessary narrow limits. It includes a heat recovery unit that helps to reduce the building's total energy demand.

Such precise control is unnecessary in the offices and social spaces. In the offices there is a fan-coil system that allows recirculation of air and

provides the occupants with local control over their environment. The volume of air delivered to the restaurant and auditorium varies in response to the number of people in those areas at different times.

Integration and concealment

A combination of the classical tradition and the pragmatism of the Chicago School has demonstrably influenced the overall form and tectonic method of the building, but architectural theory and culture had to be reconciled with a technically demanding environmental brief. Provision for services is made in four vertical risers at the four corners of the gallery spaces. Horizontal service distribution, concealed in the floor and ceiling construction, is carried from these. Such a simple, rational arrangement is strikingly similar to that of a modern office building.

↑
The main entrance
stair from the east.

↑
Upper-level
vestibule.

→
The clarity of form
and detail in the
permanent exhibition
galleries conceals the
complexity of the
services installation
that sustains them.

Within the public areas of the building, vestibules and galleries, the suspended ceiling serves as the principal, discreet expression of environmental services. In the temporary exhibition galleries and the foyers, the gridded ceilings, whose dimensions are derived from the building's geometric order, allow for precise organization of the apparatus of artificial lighting, air grilles and fire safety systems. The permanent exhibition galleries, with their translucent glass vaults, make reference to the lengthy tradition of the rooflit art museum, from Sir John Soane through Schinkel to Louis Kahn – and even to Robert Venturi's reinterpretation of Soane's Dulwich Picture Gallery at the National Gallery in London.

In their calm uniformity, the temporary and permanent exhibition spaces also call to mind the image of Mies van der Rohe's Museum for a Small City project. In the central atrium Kleihues creates a delicate illusion by installing a strip of diffused artificial light around the bases of each of the two roof pyramids. This visually detaches the roof from the orthogonal structure below.

Since the roof of the building is overlooked from the adjacent skyscrapers, the nature and location of the rooftop elements of the environmental plant needed careful thought. All the major elements have been placed beneath the roof surface, with only the essential terminals being visible from above. These are organized symmetrically in relation to the gallery rooflights and the pyramids of the atrium.

Conclusion

The Chicago museum is a highly serviced building with a demanding environmental programme. Its compact form, sealed envelope, controlled areas of glazing and comprehensive mechanical systems define it, according to our taxonomy, as environmentally exclusive. From the environmental standpoint, the design has comprehensively integrated a coherent architectural philosophy with the technical demands of the brief. It is in this respect that the architect has most demonstrably reconciled the conventions and discipline of the classical tradition with the pragmatism of the Chicago School.

Walsall Art Gallery

Caruso St John
Walsall, UK
2000

The art museum has played a significant role in the history of environmental design. For example, as noted in the introduction to this book, John Soane's Dulwich Picture Gallery (1811–14) was an example of the architect's deep interest in applying early methods of central heating, and the building is equally important in establishing a strategy for the controlled illumination of paintings by natural light. The manipulation of the cross-section in order to establish a precise relationship between work of art, viewer and light source has become a paradigm for the design of the art museum that has survived to the present day. Louis Kahn's Kimbell Museum (1972) and Renzo Piano's designs for the Menil Collection at Houston (1987) and the Beyeler Museum in Basel (1997) represent a continuation of the tradition.

This model was challenged, however, by Mies van der Rohe's project for the Museum for a Small City (1943), where a 'universal' and uniform environment for art is proposed, exploiting the potential of totally controlled artificial lighting. The vision of a new kind of gallery space was realized in Mies's National Gallery in Berlin (1958), where the major artificially lit galleries are located in the windowless crypt beneath the transparent entrance pavilion.

Since the 1960s a new demand has been placed upon the designers of art museums, following the discovery of the extent to which paintings can be physically damaged by exposure to light. Research has shown how works in all media are affected by both the intensity of the illumination to which they are exposed and the duration of exposure. Paintings can also be damaged by the quality of air in a gallery. These findings have brought about a major review of gallery design, with the result that the

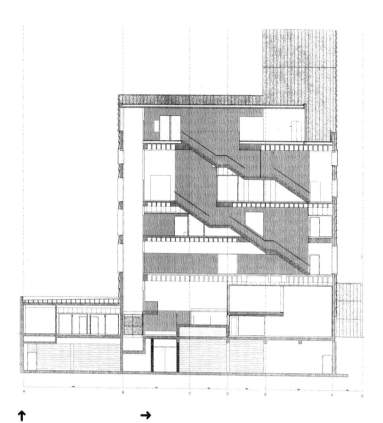

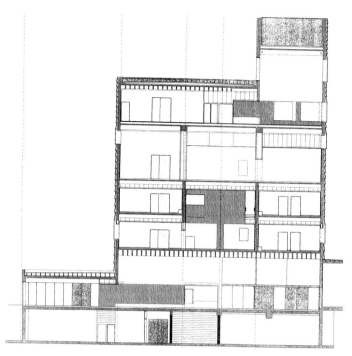

↑
The complex cross-sections, with their exposed structure and construction, suggest little of the conventions of structure-service relationships.

→
The plans show the clear distinction between the cellular structure of the Garman Ryan Collection and the less specific arrangement of the temporary exhibition galleries. They also show the vital vertical service cores.

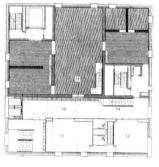

modern urban art museum has, in almost all instances, become an exercise in the exclusive mode of environmental design.

Robert Venturi developed a critique of gallery design in which he argued that the articulation of the cross-section as the principal element of daylight control has, over time, become as much a symbol of the art museum as it is necessarily functional.[1] In his design for the Sainsbury Wing in London's National Gallery (1990), Venturi paid homage to Soane by constructing a sequence of Dulwich-like galleries. But, in response to the central urban location and the environmental demands of art conservation, the form derived from historical precedent is enclosed within an envelope that renders the form more scenographic than functional.

The Walsall environment
In 1996 Caruso St John won a competition for the design of the Walsall Art Gallery. The programme required specific gallery spaces for the permanent display of the Garman Ryan collection of paintings and sculpture, as well as galleries for temporary exhibitions. The site is in the centre of this industrial town, adjacent to a canal basin and close to the main shopping centre and the bus and train stations. It is also close to a number of still-functioning factories, and there is a relatively high level of atmospheric pollution. It was part of the brief that the air delivered to the exhibition rooms had be filtered to reduce the levels of acidic gases to 20 times less than those found outside.

It is impossible to design an art gallery without defining the nature of the exhibition spaces, but there are

many other factors to take into account. In the Walsall Art Gallery there were requirements for education rooms, artists' studios, a library, a café, a shop and administrative offices. Environmentally, this has been acknowledged in the adoption of a *mixed mode* strategy, that is part *exclusive* and part *selective*. The galleries and art store are air-conditioned, with close control of temperature and humidity. The conference room is comfort cooled. The lavatories are mechanically ventilated. All other areas are naturally ventilated. In the galleries the difference between displaying a specific collection such as the Garman Ryan and providing for the inevitable diversity of temporary exhibitions is emphatically registered in the arrangement, materiality and

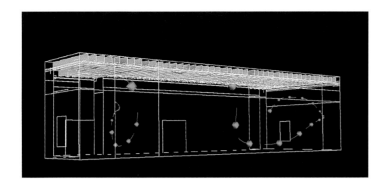
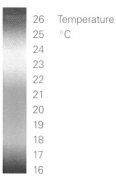

← Computer-generated representation of summer air movements.

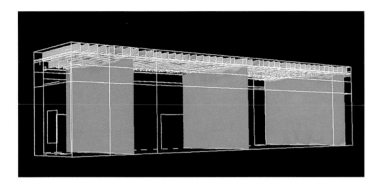
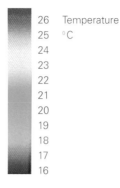

← Computer-generated representation of vertical sections, showing summer air temperature distribution.

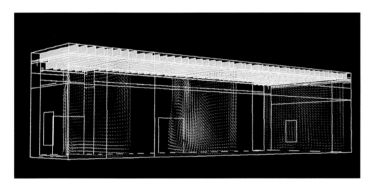
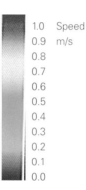

← Computer-generated representation of vertical sections, showing summer air velocity distribution.

fenestration of the respective parts of the building.

The Garman Ryan collection consists of pictures in all media – oils, watercolours, engravings and drawings – and sculpture, again in a range of materials and techniques. Most of the works are relatively small and a condition of their donation to the town was that they should be displayed in defined thematic groupings. The architects' response to this was to create a two-storey 'house' in which a series of quite small galleries was planned around a double-height space located on the first and second floors of the five-storey building. The height of the rooms – 3m (10ft) from floor to ceiling – is relatively modest, and each room has at least one window. The floors and suspended ceilings are made of Douglas fir and the walls are white-painted plaster. In both scale and material, these rooms allude to a domestic setting.

Arup's lighting design in these rooms achieves the illusion of domestic space through the careful design and positioning of the windows, but the stainless-steel and etched-glass 'laylights' are the principal source of illumination. The conservation lighting design is based on the 'kilolux hour per year' principle. This is a calculation of the cumulative exposure of the art works over a year and, in this installation, allows the diverse media to co-exist in the same room without risk to the more delicate works. The artificial lighting operates in response to the level of daylight entering the windows: levels are automatically adjusted, and white blinds are raised or lowered to control the amount of daylight that enters. Individual works can be highlighted by spotlights fixed to the laylights.

Externally, an almost continuous band of glazing is the most obvious symbol of the building's purpose. This is the clerestorey window, which is the primary source of light in the temporary galleries. Located on the third floor, these are essentially neutral spaces, waiting to receive whatever works might constitute a travelling exhibition. But, as in the Garman Ryan galleries, first appearances are deceptive. The clerestorey is a complex mechanism of environmental control. Between its outer double skin and its inner single skin of etched glass, there are artificial light fittings and motorized blinds that allow the control of light levels to meet the requirements of a particular exhibition. Blinds are adjusted

← Temporary exhibition gallery, with the exposed concrete structure above the translucent clerestory lighting.

→ The temporary exhibition galleries under construction. The framed structure at the centre of the plan provides essential flexibility for the installation of the mechanical systems.

constantly to maintain the required levels, and the artificial lighting responds to daylight levels. At night the clerestorey becomes a giant luminaire, lighting up the galleries and shining out above the town. Spotlighting for individual works is provided from points within the ribbed concrete ceiling. In the second largest gallery, the clerestorey occupies the space above the two shorter walls – but this is another illusion, since only one of these is an outer wall: the clerestorey in the other wall is an artificial light source.

In the tradition of the rooflit gallery, the golden rule is to locate the light source outside the field of vision of the viewer when he or she is looking at a work of art. The clerestorey window almost always contradicts the rule, thereby producing an unacceptable glare. The Walsall design

seeks to overcome this through a singular clerestorey design, in which the glazing acts to diffuse light, and the internal blinds act to reduce the contrast between the window and the wall below, and the narrow proportions of the spaces produce a relatively uniform distribution of the light. This is not technological determinism. In terms of Venturi's critique, the balance of symbol and function has been redefined.

Thermal conditions in the gallery spaces and the meeting rooms are maintained by the use of full air-conditioning, which keeps the internal air within strict limits of temperature, humidity and filtration. The background noise level of gallery spaces is, conventionally, kept low and this was a further factor in the design of the plant. Computational fluid dynamic (CFD) modelling was

used to evaluate the design.

The architects held strong views on preserving the carefully crafted construction and materiality of the building and sought to conceal all the principal service systems. Two main service risers run vertically through the full height of the building, but, because of the complexity of the planning, the secondary distribution is more pragmatic. There are, however, absolutely lucid strategies for the distribution of air in the gallery spaces. In the rooms of the Garman Ryan collection, the Douglas-fir-clad suspended ceilings conceal the supply ductwork. Extract air is returned to the risers using the ceiling void. Incoming air is delivered around the long sides of the laylights and is extracted through slots cut into the ceiling. The temporary exhibition galleries have exposed ribbed-

↑
Temporary exhibition gallery with major services installations, before fixing of cladding to steel studwork.

Garman Ryan Gallery showing services installations during construction.

↑
Temporary exhibition gallery after enclosure of structural frame with steel stud-frame construction.

concrete ceilings that prohibit any technical installation at high level. The ductwork is accommodated by a concrete frame structure at the core of the plan at this level, which allows the walls between the galleries to be constructed from steel stud frames and become, in effect, large service voids. Air is supplied through long slots at the top of the walls and extracted through the clerestorey windows.

In the *selective* mode areas of the building, such as the circulation spaces, the shop and the café, underfloor heating is installed under the powerfloat concrete floors. In other areas, a relatively conventional central heating system, with radiators or floor trench heaters, has been installed. Natural ventilation is provided, where appropriate, by openable windows. Elsewhere there

are high-level motorized windows, in keeping with the architects' desire to maintain the clarity of their tectonic language.

Conclusion

This building occupies an interesting position in the annals of environmental architecture. The overriding concerns of the architects belong to a world of subtle allusion and metaphor. As Brian Carter has observed, the abstract language of its form, spatiality and materiality carry references to the particularly English strand in Renaissance architecture that reached its height in Robert Smythson's Hardwick Hall (1597).[2] That building is amenable to an explicit environmental interpretation, but here at Walsall it is not that which is important.[3] We are far removed from the tradition of environmental

determinism.

In a building such as this, the job of the environmental consultant is to engineer solutions to an extremely complex programme in ways that support the poetic intentions of the architects and, crucially, are consistent with their tectonic objectives. Perhaps the closest analogy is with the collaborations between the architects and engineers of the 19th century, Soane with Perkins and Barry with Reid. As they sought to define the concept of the environmental function of buildings, these men achieved a remarkable synthesis of art and technology that was as inventive and undogmatic as the Walsall environment.

The entrance to the building is set beneath a spectacular two-way cantilever.

A computer-generated representation of the illumination of a temporary exhibition gallery.

The central space of the Garman Ryan Gallery. The timber ceilings conceal the principal services installations.

Distant view along the canal.

Tate Modern
Herzog & de Meuron
London, UK
2000

→
Night view across the
River Thames.

'Those wishing to grasp the full compass of the arts must, in addition to notions, also possess a perceptiveness trained to understand their various creative spheres. The Tate Modern is divided into two parts: a "vast void" and a space containing the art collection. The eye is led along a path through a succession of perfectly laid out spaces in which vanishing points, atmosphere and colour vary as required. All the technology is invisible. Without being an expressive force, the technology is what it ought to be: simply a service. The interdisciplinary approach creates a constant dialogue between architecture and art, and a harmonious synthesis within a historical monument regained to inject life into an area through the dynamics of culture.'

In this statement about their design for Tate Modern, the Swiss architects Herzog & de Meuron establish the essential continuity of art, architecture and context that defines the essence of their interpretation of the programme for the building.[1] They stress their 'interdisciplinary' approach and make clear their position on technology, emphatically declaring that it should be 'simply a

↓
East–west section,
looking north through
the turbine hall.

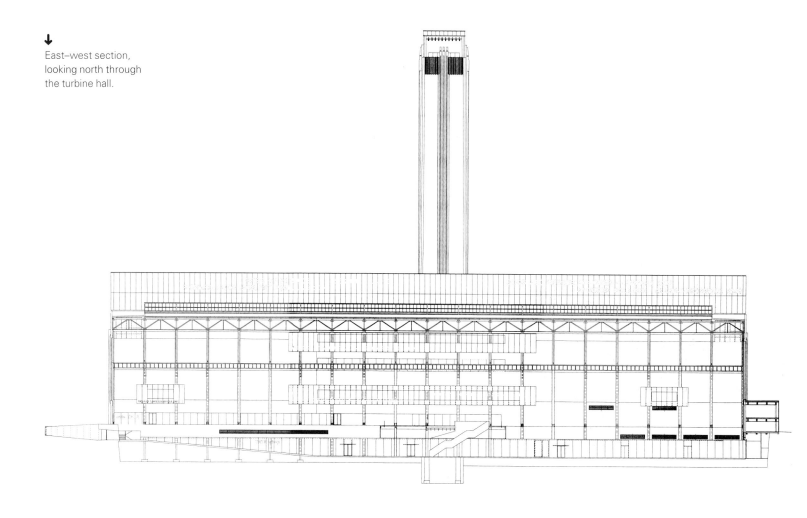

service'. In the same discussion the architects made some forthright comments about contemporary British architecture, describing it as 'all straightforward in the Gothic tradition. Architecture, they think here, always has to give expression to the technical side. We found that out time and time again in the form of a cultural confrontation during the building phase.'

Power to art

The London Borough of Southwark has a rich history.[2] By the 19th century it was a major industrial area packed with factories, wharves and dense slum housing. This contrasted with the wealth and grandeur of the City of London on the opposite bank of the River Thames – a state of affairs that persisted through much of the 20th century. In 1947 Bankside power

station was designed by Sir Giles Gilbert Scott to provide electricity supplies for much of the City. It opened in 1963 and was decommissioned in 1981. In 1994, the disused building was chosen as the site of Tate Modern – a location for the display of the Tate Gallery's collection of international modern art as well as for temporary exhibitions. The development of Tate Modern helped to transform this area of the south bank of the Thames into a major cultural centre close to the City.

Scott's vast brick-clad structure has become one of London's major landmarks. His design gave powerful expression to the building's utilitarian function through its symmetrical composition, with a single chimney gathering the flues from an array of boilers placed at the centre of the river frontage – where it acts as

counterpoint to the dome of St Paul's Cathedral on the opposite bank. Inside the building were two full-height volumes, the boiler house and the turbine hall, both of which ran the full length of the northern part of the building. A third major element, the switch house, offers space to accommodate the expected expansion of the museum.

Plan and section

The volume of the boiler house and turbine hall together was 160m (525ft) long, 54m (177ft) wide, and 34m (112ft) from basement to roof. After the surviving generating plant had been removed, the differentiation between the two major spaces was retained. The turbine hall was opened up to its full height and becomes an enormous covered public space, entered by a sweeping ramp leading

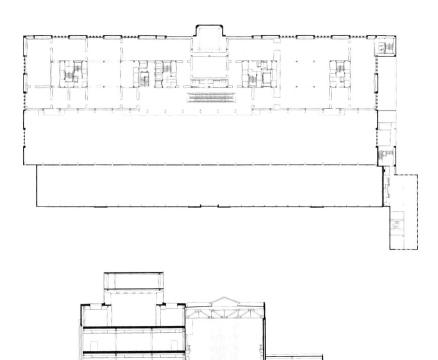

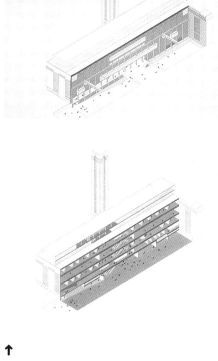

↑
Cut-away
axonometrics

↑
Gallery floor plan, showing the relation of gallery spaces to service cores and circulation.

Cross-section, looking east, showing the turbine hall (centre) with the gallery spaces inserted within the former boiler house.

down from the western entrance. To the north, at the foot of the chimney, is a second entrance approached from the river frontage. A seven-storey steel structure has been inserted into the boiler house to form the art museum itself. This rises above the brick mass of the power station to emerge as a translucent 'light beam', signalling the building's new function across the London skyline. The internal façade between the gallery and concourse holds a composition of similarly translucent 'light boxes'.

Within the seven-storey section the galleries are at levels 3, 4 and 5, and the other elements of the museum – shop, lecture theatre, administrative offices, cafés and restaurant – are below, at levels 1 and 2, or above, at levels 6 and 7. The galleries at levels 3 and 5 contain works from the Tate's permanent collection and level 4 is

designated for temporary exhibitions. Within the gallery areas, the internal subdivision is formed by wide hollow partitions faced in medium-density fibreboard. The principal circulation and service spaces rise through the central part of the plan and open out into concourses that overlook the turbine hall at each level.

Form and environment

Arup's environmental design strategy is based on the architects' decree that the technology of the building should be 'simply a service'. In developing this position further, they pointed to the power exerted over them by the existing building: 'whenever we departed – in the dialectically anticipatory sense – from what was there, that became in a sense quite ridiculous, because the existing fabric was always stronger'.

The gallery spaces have a precisely calculated set of relationships with the existing fabric. Levels 3 and 4 occupy the volume defined by Scott's huge windows to north, east and west. At level 5 the perimeter galleries sit beneath the parapet of the former boiler house, from where they are lit by concealed rooflights, and the central spaces penetrate up into the lower part of the 'light beam'. This defines two strips of continuous clerestory window, facing north and south.

The lighting design of the spaces follows directly from these relationships between old and new. The aim was to bring daylight into the galleries wherever possible and to balance this with the needs for control and conservation and the need to provide supplementary artificial lighting. At level 5 the rooflights of the

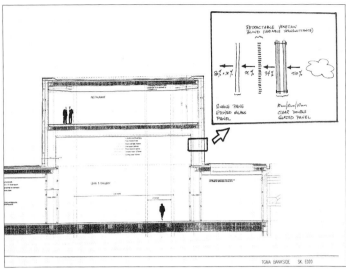

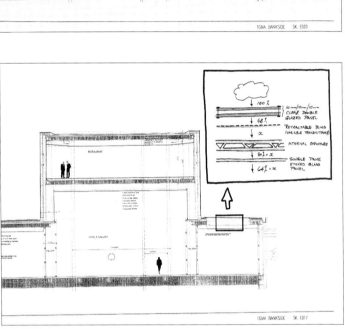

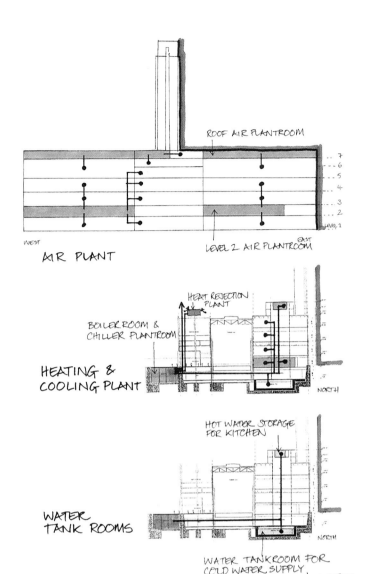

perimeter galleries have diffusing 'laylights' of translucent glass. Concealed blinds control levels when there is an excess of daylight and there is artificial lighting for use on dull days and at night. The clerestories in the central double-height galleries have a double layer of translucent glazing. In the void between the layers, adjustable louvred blinds control the level of daylight that is admitted and artificial lighting provides night-time illumination. Artificial lighting also illuminates the 'light beam' as it glows above the museum's rooftop at night. At levels 3 and 4, daylight enters through Scott's windows – 'cathedral' windows, as Herzog & de Meuron describe them – supplemented by artificially lit laylights that simulate the effect of the rooflights on level 5. In all the galleries further artificial lighting can be installed, in the form of spotlights, to illuminate individual works. Opaque roller blinds allow all the windows and rooflights to be completely blacked out.

This strategy makes it possible to bring varying levels and qualities of light into each of the galleries, allowing visitors to experience a sense of the progression of the seasons and changes in the local weather. In their architectural development these spaces are elaborately unassertive. All junctions of floor and wall, wall and ceiling, clerestory or laylight and ceiling, are unadorned and flush. Sawn oak boards bring warmth and texture to the lower galleries; on the upper floor, wood is replaced by a polished concrete finish.

The turbine hall – used for temporary exhibitions of large-scale works – retains its original roof structure. The continuous central rooflight has been reconstructed and provides copious daylight. Banks of fluorescent lamps running along the blind south wall supplement this at night – but the dramatic light in this space is provided by the 'light boxes' that project from the opposite wall. By their use of translucent glass, these bring the principal material theme of the new intervention, expressed on the exterior by the light beam, into the heart of the building. The light beam plays a consciously ambiguous part in the life of the building, acting as a bringer of light during the day and as a beacon at night. The light boxes also have dual functions – as inhabited space, extending the galleries and concourses into the turbine hall, and as enormous luminaires.

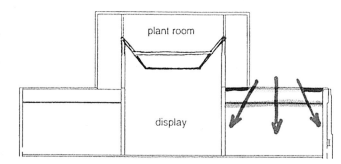

←

Engineer's design drawings, showing detailed explorations of specific conditions of the enclosure in the exhibition galleries (far left, top and bottom) and schematic layouts of the air plant, heating and cooling plant and water services (left).

↓
Computer-generated studies of relative humidity in exhibition spaces

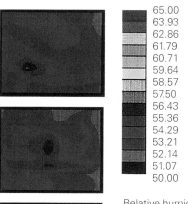

| 65.00 |
| 63.93 |
| 62.86 |
| 61.79 |
| 60.71 |
| 59.64 |
| 58.57 |
| 57.50 |
| 56.43 |
| 55.36 |
| 54.29 |
| 53.21 |
| 52.14 |
| 51.07 |
| 50.00 |

Relative humidity in percentages.

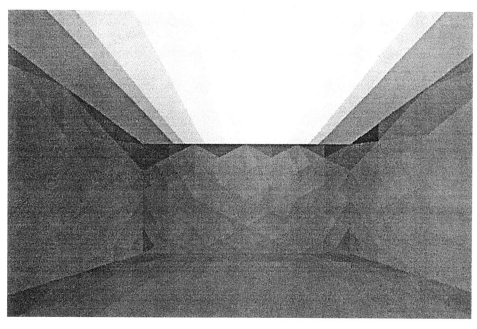

↑
Daylighting studies of roof-lit gallery.

Invisible service

Designing the environment of an art museum is not solely a question of controlled lighting. Modern standards of conservation demand that, almost without exception, works of art must be displayed in spaces where every measurable element of the environment is controlled. The envelope of the modern gallery is a sealed box – exclusive, in our terminology – within which mechanical systems operate to admit, filter, temper, supply and extract air at precisely calculated levels of temperature, humidity and cleanliness. To achieve this, a building must incorporate extensive networks of ducts and voids connecting every conditioned space to centrally located plant rooms.

The architectural philosophy of Herzog & de Meuron eschews what they identify as a particularly British preoccupation: 'to give expression to the technical side'. For them, 'All the technology is invisible.' In Tate Modern, the air-conditioning to the galleries is a low-velocity displacement system. The supply air is carried from the plant room through the vertical service cores and is then distributed horizontally at each floor at high level. From there it travels downwards, in ducts located within the hollow walls that define the sequence of galleries. A plenum space extends beneath the floors, and air is finally delivered from this to the galleries through cast-iron grilles. Return air is extracted through the ceiling void. To achieve efficient distribution and to limit the depth of the structural and servicing zone, a double slab section was devised: a second slab was placed 460mm (18in) above the main concrete floor slab, creating the supply plenum.

The cast-iron grilles, set into floors of either sawn oak or polished concrete, are a carefully thought-out element of the iconography of the building and, in particular, of the architects' position on the visual status of the services installations. 'The building has, first of all, this roughness. That's why we took these grilles. Without creating industrial architecture in the strict sense. There's more at issue here than just moods...but architecture does have to do with atmospheres and images. If I have smooth aluminium grilles, for example, then I want to demonstrate that we have a ventilation system which contrasts with the stuffy old industrial building. And with these cast-iron grilles, I blur this question of old and new, I don't even ask it.'[3]

The turbine hall, with
sculpture installation
by Louise Bourgeois.

Detail of cast-iron air
conditioning grille set
in sawn oak floor.

At certain critical points in the building the doctrine of 'invisible technology' has been abandoned. The most notable of these is in the circulation concourses, where the suspended ceiling has been omitted to reveal the network of black-painted air ducts and electrical conduits beneath the exposed concrete slab. A similar, but perhaps more self-consciously ironic installation is to be found in the café, where haloes of fluorescent light are suspended beneath an array of exposed machinery, this time finished in metallic silver paint.

Conclusion

In transforming Bankside power station into Tate Modern, Herzog & de Meuron challenged the specifically British interpretation of the relationship between architecture and technology, the approach that they characterize as 'all straightforward in the Gothic tradition', where architecture, 'give[s] expression to the technical side'. Although the roots of this tradition may be traced back to the material theories of John Ruskin and Augustus Pugin, in the lineage proposed by Nikolaus Pevsner in *Pioneers of Modern Design*, equal authority for a kind of technological display may be found in the European traditions of Henri Labrouste and Gottfried Semper.[4] More recently, Franco Albini's works and Louis Kahn's strictures about 'ducts and pipes' indicate its universal diffusion.

The wider perspective offered by our historical review of the relationship between the architecture and engineering of environment may more specifically locate Herzog & de Meuron's position in the tradition of, in Banham's terminology, 'concealed power'. That interpretation, as explained in the introduction, runs through the unfolding of this history over the last two centuries, alongside the alternative of 'exposed power', in the work of architects as different as Karl Friedrich Schinkel, Mies van der Rohe and Robert Venturi. It is in this context that the subtle clarity of the engineering of this design makes its greatest contribution.

← Detail of internal façade of turbine hall.

→ Concourse at Level 5. The omission of a suspended ceiling in the circulation areas provides one of the few occasions in the building where services are exposed to public view.

↓ Exhibition gallery at Level 5, with clerestory lighting flowing from the externally expressed light beam.

Portuguese Pavilion
Expo 98
Álvaro Siza
Lisbon, Portugal
1998

→
The entrance canopy
provides a protected
microclimate before
entering the building.

'Working in a team is like working alone, but with a capacity for analysis and invention multiplied by X,' writes the architect Álvaro Siza.[1] 'Each person's discoveries, each hypothesis launched into the flow, generate further hypotheses and further discoveries on their part and other's – as happens with my ideas when I work alone – but here at a giddy rate.... It is therefore urgent, not least for the work of these agents, that we extend information early on and to everyone, to bring to an end the myths of specialisation, of the incommunicable complexity of all the different specialisms.'

Admiration for the work of Álvaro Siza focuses on the way in which his buildings appear to transform the tenets of international Modernism into a decorous and culturally grounded vocabulary that is responsive to the issues of globalization. As Kenneth Frampton writes, 'Siza pursues an architecture of resistance. The global has always to be offset by the local at every level, not in terms of some categoric rejection of universal technology, but rather in recognition of the need to mediate technique through culture.'[2] In view of his pronounced sensitivity to context, it is surprising that little

critical attention has been given to Siza as an environmentalist. He regards teamwork as crucial to the success of contemporary architecture, and his design for the Portuguese Pavilion at Expo 98 makes an important contribution to the developing relationship between architecture and environmental engineering.

Site and programme
In addition to its function as an international showground, Expo 98 played a role in the planned expansion of Lisbon. The site on derelict land to the north of the

213

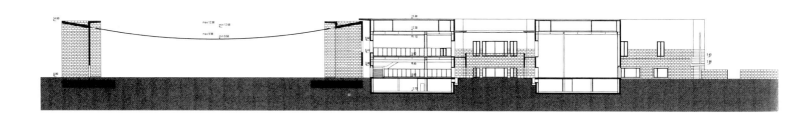

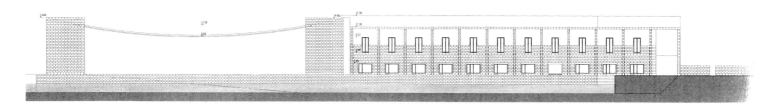

historic centre, on the banks of the Tagus, is close to the international airport and on the main railway route to Coimbra and Porto. As part of the preparations for Expo 98, the metro system, which in recent years has transformed the city's transport infrastructure, was extended to the site. Santiago Calatrava's remarkable Oriente Station – which marks a meeting point of metro, main railway and local bus network – links the Expo site directly to local, regional, national and international transport networks, laying the foundations for major expansion. At the time of Expo 98 a major retail and commercial centre had already been completed and a start had been made on a residential development programme.

The Portuguese Pavilion was designed symbolically and functionally to represent the host

nation and to provide a venue for all the important ceremonies that took place during Expo 98. It was also the location of a major multimedia installation designed by Eduardo Souto de Moura. The pavilion occupies a spectacular position overlooking the lagoon of Doca dos Olivais at the centre of the Expo site. Its form is both simple and remarkable. A two-storey pavilion faced in stone and stucco stands to the north of an independently supported entrance canopy whose scale and construction are awe-inspiring. A shallow concrete catenary hangs on steel cables between two stone- and tile-clad supporting structures, spanning 67.5m (221ft). The space defined becomes, simultaneously, piazza, providing a microclimate sheltered from the summer sun, and porte cochère,

signalling the entrance to a important public building.

Indeterminacy and environmental design

Uncertainty about the long-term use of the building was a major factor in its design, which might have led towards an architecture of overt 'adaptability'. The apparatus of 'free space' and its concomitant of 'flexible services' have played a major part in recent architectural methodology. The arguments that underpinned the design of a building such as the Centre Pompidou might have been brought to bear on the Portuguese Pavilion. As *The Architectural Review* wrote of Pompidou, 'nothing is rigid, immutable, the container is flexible, adaptable through the use of "soft" mechanisms, articulated so that it can be adapted'.[3]

Conceptual sketch
showing the
relationship between
the sweeping canopy
and the body of the
building.

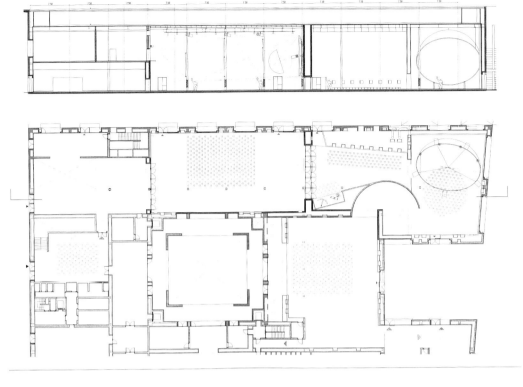

Longitudinal section
through the building
showing the internal
courtyard.

↑

Ground floor plan.

←

South elevation.

With two comprehensive internal refits since its completion, the Centre Pompidou appears to have been well served by such an approach to its design. But Siza's architecture is not concerned with the kind of functional openness and technological display represented by the Centre Pompidou; in his eyes, if the future role of a building is uncertain, a less demonstrative solution has to found.

The pavilion is organized around an open atrium. Io the west and north are the main double-height exhibition spaces, with the more cellular ceremonial spaces and services occupying the two-storeyed south and east wings. The structure of the building is a hybrid of reinforced-concrete external envelope with a steel frame within supporting lightweight concrete on profiled steel decking to form the slabs. This

solution was devised by the engineers in response to the seismic risk in the Lisbon region and also to allow removal of floors and partitions if that became part of a replanning strategy in the future.

To meet the demands for comfort during summer ceremonies, the building is air-conditioned, but the envelope and mechanical systems are integrated to make its operation both efficient and adaptable. The inhabited spaces arc sandwiched between an extensive basement and an array of rooftop plant enclosures concealed behind a continuous high parapet. The perimeter walls and the walls around the atrium are double-skinned and become, from a services point of view, continuous voids containing all the service systems, including the air supply and extract ducts. These walls also provide the structural stability of

the building, allowing flexibility of internal planning. The complete integration of architectural, structural and environmental needs is testimony to the relationship between the architect and Arup.

The body of the building is punctured with small window openings that are deeply recessed into the double-skin construction, giving some protection against solar gains, while adjustable external shutters give complete solar exclusion if this becomes necessary. To the east the façade is further sheltered by an oversailing arcade that forms a grand walkway alongside the Doca dos Olivais. The proportion and disposition of the fenestration set in the thermally massive enclosure is a clear response to the climate and architectural traditions of Lisbon and its region and, also, a demonstration

215

←

The canopy forms at once a piazza and a porte cochère, signalling the entrance to an important building.

→

Schematic elevation showing the relative position and dimension of the fenestration of the south façade and the mechanical systems.

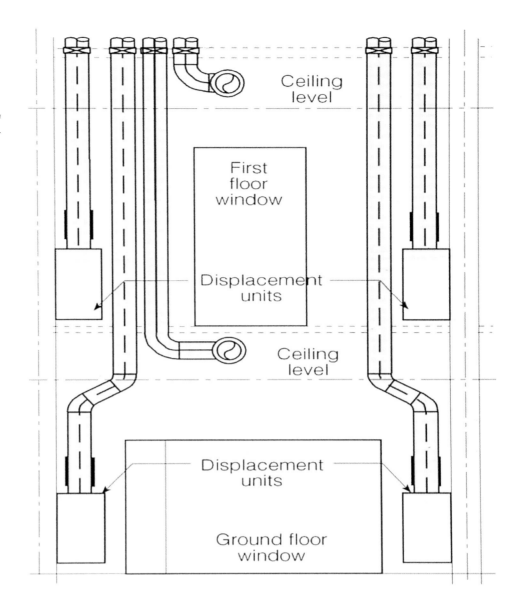

Ceiling level

First floor window

Displacement units

Ceiling level

Displacement units

Ground floor window

of Frampton's proposition of Siza's mediation of 'technique through culture'.

A combined heat and power (CHP) system delivers heated and chilled water and electricity to all the main buildings at the Expo site. Within the Portuguese Pavilion heat exchangers are used to transfer the energy delivered to the building's own water circuits. These supply heating and cooling to seven separate air-handling units housed in the rooftop plant spaces. Each of these units controls a distinct vertical zone of the building through ductwork concealed in the double skin.

Supply ducts are carried down to low-level displacement units concealed within the wall at each floor. These deliver conditioned air to each space, which is extracted by displacement at high level, from where it is returned to

the plant room by a system of ducts, again hidden in the wall voids. All these systems are discreetly incorporated in the refined layering and restrained detail of Siza's interiors.

Conclusion

In terms of our 'environmental taxonomy', this building is located towards, respectively, the exclusive and concealed ends of the two principal axes, exclusive/selective mode and concealed/exposed power. It is a highly serviced structure in which the external enclosure acts to hold at bay the effects of extremes of climate, in particular the heat of the summer, in order to minimize demands on the mechanical plant. Equally, it succeeds in subtly integrating an extensive array of plant into its structure and fabric.

One of the themes in Álvaro Siza's

work throughout his career has been a concern with the expression of consistency rather than that which is conspicuously new. 'After years of passionate invention, of separation from History...after the Modernist movement, a reading, albeit transitory, of the huge amount we have received from the previous generation seems fairly clear to me,' he writes. 'In spite of new materials and new techniques...the essence of Architecture has not changed.'[4] The achievement of the Portuguese Pavilion has two sides to it. A collaboration of architect and consultants has led to a synthesis and organization of structure and services that is as coherent as Louis Kahn's distinction between 'served' and 'servant', but which is subsumed into form and language that are subtly related to context and culture.

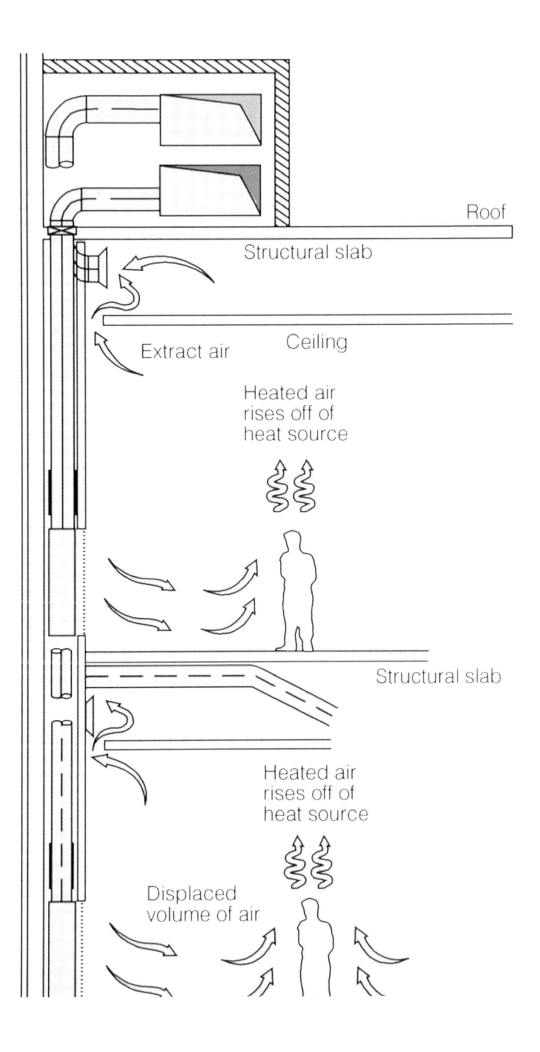

Roof

Structural slab

Extract air

Ceiling

Heated air
rises off of
heat source

Structural slab

Heated air
rises off of
heat source

Displaced
volume of air

←

Technical cross-
section showing the
relationship of
structure and
servicing
installations. The
intention is to achieve
maximum efficiency
with concealed
power systems.

↑ Gallery space.   → Internal courtyard.

← First-floor reception room, showing relationship with the internal courtyard.

↑ Furniture and murals by Álvaro Siza.

Velodrome
Dominique Perrault
Berlin, Germany
1997

Plan view of model,
showing velodrome
and swimming pool,
set in the raised
plinth with its orchard
of Normandy
apple trees.

Track cycling is both an outdoor and an indoor sport. In its early days, when cycling was a predominantly European passion, there was a clear distinction between the summer and winter versions. Summer events, which often included the sprint finish of a road race, were usually staged in large outdoor arenas such as the Parc de Princes in Paris, and the short-track winter meetings, which often took the form of six-day team races, were indoors. There were a few permanent indoor tracks – the best known was probably Vel d'Hiv in Paris, now demolished – but in many cases these events took place on temporarily erected circuits within large exhibition halls, for example. As a consequence, the tracks varied enormously in size and quality. In recent years the sport has become much more popular and there have been moves to standardize tracks. New tracks have been built around the world, the majority of which are indoor, allowing year-round use.

In 1991, Berlin city council made a bid for their city, the capital of a reunited Germany, to be the venue of the 2000 Olympic Games. Work began on the development of a number of new sports installations, including a

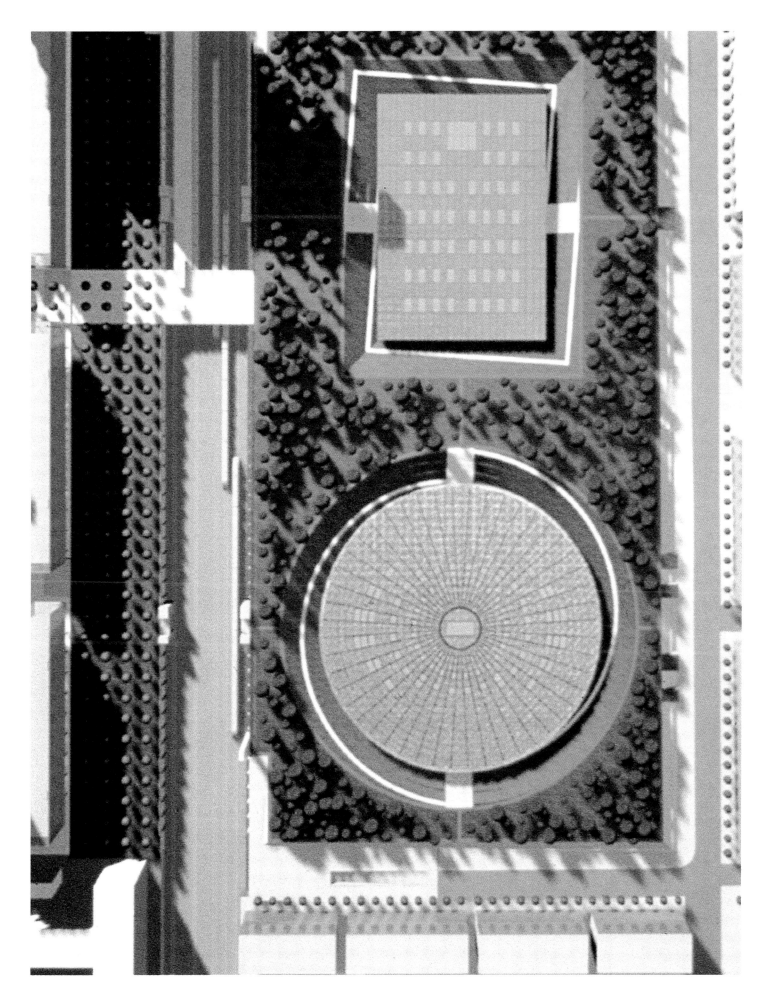

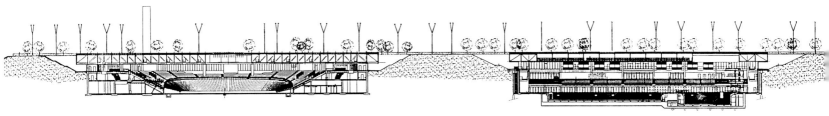

↑
Long-section, with
velodrome (left) and
swimming pool
(right).

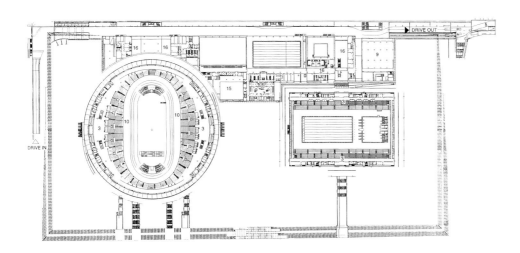

←
The plan shows the
connection between
the two primary
arenas and the
shared service zones
beneath the plinth.

velodrome and swimming pool
complex on a site in the
Prenzlauerberg district in Berlin's
former eastern zone. The Paris-based
architect Dominique Perrault won an
international competition for the
project, held in 1992. As concrete
evidence of Berlin's commitment to
the Olympics, the project moved
quickly to site. The Berlin Olympic bid
was ultimately unsuccessful, but the
project continued to completion of the
velodrome in 1997 and completion of
the swimming pool a year later.

Perrault's design puts the entire
building below ground level. In the
open, Modernist structure of
Prenzlauerberg, with its ranks of high-
rise apartments and commercial
buildings, he has created an 'orchard'
of Normandy apple trees in which the
roof planes of the two sports halls
resemble glistening lakes, one

circular, the other rectangular. Each
consists of a concrete-lined
excavation covered by a large-span
steel roof. The entire roof plane and
the edges of each enclosure are
covered in a fine steel mesh whose
appearance constantly changes with
the light.

The sporting environment
A sports building has to provide
comfortable conditions for both
athletes and spectators. Regulating
temperature, ventilation, lighting and
acoustics is more complex in such a
place than in many other building
types. The Berlin Six-Day cycle race,
held each year in January, has
sessions each day from six o'clock in
the evening until three o'clock in the
morning. As the two-man teams race
around the track, a crowd of up to
13,000 fills the perimeter seating and

the central piste, and a carnival takes
place as the cyclists circle around. The
demands this places on the
environmental systems of the
building are easy to imagine. In
addition to its primary function as the
venue for cycling, the velodrome is
also used for other sports, such as
tennis, concerts, both classical and
pop, trade shows, political rallies – all
of which add to the environmental
brief. The continental climate of Berlin
has long cold winters, with
temperatures often down to -15°C
(5°F), and hot summers, when
temperatures as high as 35°C (95°F)
may be experienced.

In Perrault's design, the circular roof
structure hovers over an elliptical
enclosure within which is the oval
cycle track. The main body of the
building is below natural ground
level. Above this rises the plateau of

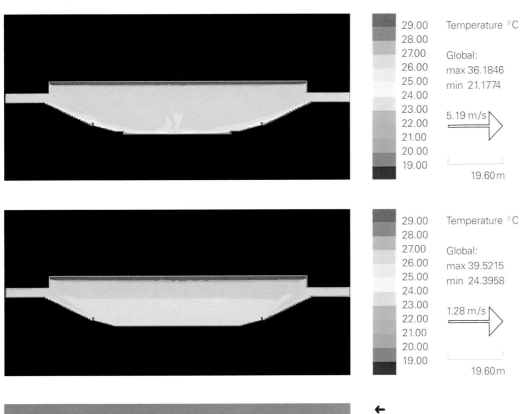

	Temperature °C
29.00	
28.00	
27.00	Global:
26.00	max 36.1846
25.00	min 21.1774
24.00	
23.00	
22.00	5.19 m/s
21.00	
20.00	
19.00	

19.60 m

Computer models, showing predicted temperature distributions in the velodrome for alternative cycling and concert configurations.

	Temperature °C
29.00	
28.00	
27.00	Global:
26.00	max 39.5215
25.00	min 24.3958
24.00	
23.00	
22.00	1.28 m/s
21.00	
20.00	
19.00	

19.60 m

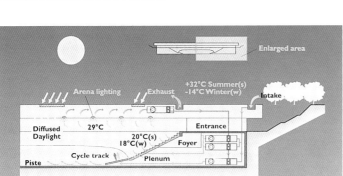

Engineer's schematic section, showing principles of the environmental strategy.

the 'orchard', and the steel-mesh cladding of the roof floats 1m (3ft) above this. The cross-section defines and articulates the essential elements of the environmental strategy. The roof disc is 140m (459ft) in diameter. It consists of 48 steel radial trusses that span from a circumferential ring of 16 concrete columns with linking trusses, and a 14.4m (47ft) radius ring truss at the centre. Each radial truss is restrained by tie-down elements at a radius of 65.2m (214ft). Secondary beams connect the trusses in both their top and bottom planes. A major feature of the design is the circular rooflight that spans the central opening, bringing a pool of natural light into the heart of the arena.

Heat

The air supply to this huge enclosure is delivered at low level, through the vertical surface of the precast-concrete steps that form the seating terraces, and at the inner rim of the cycle track. Extract is by mechanical exhaust close to the perimeter of the disc, where it does not obstruct the rooflight and is relatively unobtrusive visually. The natural buoyancy of the air assists the extraction process. This configuration is an economical means of creating a microclimate at the lower, inhabited level of the arena. Supply to the seating and the piste is from separate units. Arup's design was validated using a computational fluid dynamics (CFD) model, which allowed a series of occupancy patterns related to the potential uses of the building to be simulated for a range of climatic conditions. A centralized plant serves both the velodrome and the swimming pool. This incorporates a combined heat and power plant (CHP)

which delivers both heat and electricity. Additional heat is drawn from the district heating system that serves much of Berlin. The system is configured so that the CHP plant is used to heat the water in the swimming pool and to run the pool ventilation. It also provides emergency power.

Light

The velodrome has an extensive artificial lighting installation to allow events to be held there after dark. Illumination for the major sporting events is provided by an array of floodlights, concentrically arranged to follow the geometry of the roof structure. To achieve uniform lighting within the geometrical constraints of the architecture, the lamps were designed with asymmetric reflectors. This installation is supplemented by a

← The layered structure of the roof, showing the relation of glazing and shading.

→ Computer-generated daylighting distribution diagrams.

↓ The 140m (460ft) diameter roof under construction. The central ring truss was temporarily supported until the radial beams were all in place.

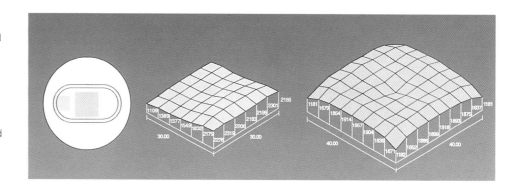

secondary set of powerful lamps to provide the higher level of light needed for televised events. Each lamp can be individually addressed by the computer control system. This makes it possible to provide appropriate lighting for all the other, non-sports events that take place in the building. Once again, computer modelling played an essential role in the design of the installation.

Sound

Acoustics may seem of secondary importance in the design of a sports building, but the noise of an enthusiastic crowd contained within an enclosure must be properly controlled. First, the response of the enclosure has to be analysed to make sure that an atmospheric but comfortable acoustic is achieved. Second, particularly in a residential

district such as Prenzlauerberg, it is important to limit the noise that is transmitted through the enclosure to the surroundings. In this case it was also necessary to achieve an acoustic that would support other uses of the space, particularly musical performances.

The form and materiality of the velodrome are determined by the needs of the sport. Perrault's elegant geometrical system of superimposed figures – circle, ellipse and oval – invests the space with a clear order. The materials of the arena, mainly concrete, are acoustically reflective. In a space such this, the roof is the main source of acoustic control. A liner tray system was suspended below the roof deck, whose construction was optimized to provide both sound insulation and low-frequency absorption. Together the deck and the

hanging system control the high- and mid-frequency reverberations, and the hanging trays optimize the low frequencies. The design achieves a reverberation time of 2.1 seconds across the frequency range, thereby avoiding the exaggeration of low frequencies often suffered in large volumes. Within the arena itself, the design was detailed to avoid focused reflection from the curved forms. Sound-absorbent materials were used wherever possible, and the continuous glazed strip above the upper seating was angled to reflect sound up onto the absorbent panels in the roof.

The acoustic needs of most kinds of performance are met by an extensive electro-acoustic installation. Three types of loudspeaker are arranged in a concentric configuration, directed respectively towards the upper

↑
Precast concrete seating tiers of the velodrome. The circular holes in the risers are the supply inlets from the air system.

↑
The perimeter of the roof disc, clad in steel mesh, floats above the perimeter concourse.

seating, lower seating and the piste area; the whole system is computer-controlled to allow it to be configured to suit each individual event. It is compatible with the powerful sound systems used by rock bands.

Conclusion

The Berlin Velodrome is one of the few modern sports arenas that transcend the pragmatics of the geometry of the playing area, the provision of acceptable sight lines for the spectators and muscular structural expression. Perrault's formal play of circle and rectangle, set into the manmade landscape of the Normandy 'orchard', is a poetic addition to the arid urban fringe of Prenzlauerberg.

The building is a wonderfully explicit demonstration of creative collaboration between architect and engineer. Central to this is the cross-sectional order that elegantly resolves the complex environmental requirements of the modern indoor sports arena. Within the sealed, exclusive envelope, the mechanical systems are physically and functionally integrated with the structure so that they deliver heat, light and sound in correct measure where and when they are needed.

←

The velodrome set
out for its secondary
use as a concert hall.
The roof structure is
seen to perform its
additional function of
integrating elements
of the environmental
services.

A major cycle race in
progress. The
computer-controlled
artificial lighting
concentrates
attention on the oval
of the track within
the circular arena.

↑

The roof structure
in detail.

Appendix

INTRODUCTION

1. Le Corbusier, *Vers unc architccturc*, Paris, 1923. English translation by Frederick Etchells, *Towards a New Architecture*, London, 1926.
2. Nikolaus Pevsner, *Pioneers of Modern Design*, revised edition, Penguin Books, Harmondsworth, 1960. First published as *Pioneers of the Modern Movement*, Faber & Faber, London, 1936.
3. Sigfried Giedion, *Space, Time and Architecture*, Harvard University Press, Cambridge, Mass., 1941. Fourth revised edition 1962.
4. Reyner Banham, *The Architecture of the Well-tempered Environment*, The Architectural Press, London, 1969.
5. T. K. Derry and Trevor I. Williams, *A Short History of Technology: from the earliest times to AD 1900*, Oxford University Press, Oxford, 1960.
6. Robert Bruegmann, 'Central Heating and Forced Ventilation: Origins and Effects on Architectural Design', *Journal of the Society of Architectural Historians*, XXXVII, 1978, pages 143–60.
7. Todd Willmert, 'Heating Methods and Their Impact on Soane's Work: Lincoln's Inn Fields and Dulwich Picture Gallery', J*ournal of the Society of Architectural Historians*, LII, 1993, pages 26–58.
8. M. H. Port (ed.), *The Houses of Parliament*, Yale University Press, New Haven, 1976.
9. John Olley, 'The Reform Club', in Dan Cruickshank (ed.), *Timeless Architecture*, The Architectural Press, London, 1985.
10. John Olley, 'St George's Hall, Liverpool, Parts One and Two, *The Architects' Journal*, 18 and 25 June 1986.
11. See Pevsner, op. cit.
12. See Giedion, op. cit.
13. See E. O. Sachs, *Modern Opera House and Theatres*, 3 vols. London, 1896–98, for a full description of this building and its installations. Sachs's work is a key reference for theatre design in the 19th century.
14. D. B. Reid, *Illustrations*, cited in Bruegmann, op. cit.
15. Fernand Léger, 'The origins of painting and its representational value', Montjoie, Paris, 1913. Reprinted in E. F. Fry, *Cubism*, Thames and Hudson, London 1966.
16. Le Corbusier, programme of *L'Esprit Nouveau* no. 1, October 1920.
17 Le Corbusier and Pierre Jeanneret, *Cinque points d'une architecture nouvelle*, 1925.
18. Brian Brace Taylor, *Le Corbusier: the City of Refuge, Paris, 1929/33*, University of Chicago Press, Chicago and London, 1987. First published as *La Cité de Refuge di Le Corbusier 1929/33*, Officina Edizione, Rome, 1978.
19. Le Corbusier, *Precisions: On the Present State of Architecture and City Planning*, English translation, MIT Press, Cambridge, Mass., 1991. First published as *Précisions sur un état de l'architecture et de l'urbanism*, Cres et Cie., Paris, 1930.

20. For a detailed account of the controversy over the performance of the executed design, see Brian Brace Taylor, op. cit.
21. See John Allen, *Berthold Lubetkin: Architecture and the Tradition of Progress*, RIBA Publications, London, 1992, for a detailed account of Lubetkin's life and work.
22. Kenneth Frampton, *Studies in Tectonic Culture: The Poetics of Construction in Nineteenth and Twentieth Century Architecture*, MIT Press, Cambridge, Mass., 1995.
23. Pierre van Meiss, 'The aesthtics of gravity: La Rinascente Department Store, Rome' in *arq*, vol. 4, no. 3, 2000, pp. 237–45.
24. See Rayner Banham, *The Architecture of the Well-tempered Environment*, The Architectural Press, London, 1969, for an outline of the environmental aspects of SCSD.
25. Louis I. Kahn, quoted in *World Architecture 1*, Studio Books, London, 1964.
26. See 'Space for services: the architectural dimension', in Dean Hawkes, *The Environmental Tradition: Studies in the Architecture of Environment*, E. & F. N. Spon, London, 1996.
27. Charles Jencks, *The Language of Post-Modern Architecture*, 4th edition, Academy Editions, London, 1984.
28. Kenneth Frampton, 'Towards a critical regionalism: six points for an architecture of resistance', in Hal Foster (ed.), *Postmodern Culture*, Pluto Press, London & Concord, Mass., 1985.
29. Dean Hawkes, 'The Sainsbury Wing, National Gallery, London', in *The Environmental Tradition: Studies in the Architecture of Environment*, E. & F. N. Spon, London, 1996.
30. W. Boesiger and H. Girsberger, *Le Corbusier 1910–1965*, Les Editions d'Architecture, Zurich, 1967.
31. Alan Colquhoun, 'Symbolic and literal aspects of technology', *Architectural Design*, November 1962, reprinted in *Essays in Architectural Criticism: Modern Architecture and Historical Change*, Oppositions Books, MIT Press, Cambridge, Mass., 1981.
32. Kenneth Frampton, *Studies in Tectonic Culture: The Poetics of Construction in Nineteenth and Twentieth Century Architecture*, MIT Press, Cambridge, Mass., 1995.
33. T. K. Derry and Trevor I. Williams, op. cit.
34. See Introduction to Dean Hawkes, *The Environmental Tradition: Studies in the Architecture of Environment*, E. & F. N. Spon, London, 1996, for a detailed account of the derivation of this proposition.
35. Victor Olgyay, *Design with Climate*, Princeton University Press, Princeton, 1963.
36. See Philip Steadman, *Energy, Environment and Building*, Cambridge University Press, Cambridge, for a comprehensive summary of these early designs.
37. A pioneering autonomous project was the Cambridge Autonomous House Project. See *Architectural Design*, November 1974. The work of Brenda and Robert Vale, *The New Autonomous*

House: Design and Planning for Sustainability, Thames and Hudson, London, 2000, has carried these principles into built reality.
38. Thomas Herzog (ed.), *Solar Energy in Architecture and Urban Planning*, Prestel, Munich and New York, 1996, brings together an extensive and representative sample of these designs.
39. See Robert Powell, *Ken Yeang: Rethinking the Environmental Filter*, foreword by Kisho Kurokawa, Landmark Press, Singapore, 1989; and Ken Yeang, *The Green Skyscraper: The Basis for Designing Sustainable Intensive Buildings*, Prestel, New York, 1999.
40. See Dean Hawkes, 'Building shape and energy use', an essay first published in 1980 and reprinted in revised form in *The Environmental Tradition: Studies in the Architecture of Environment*, E. & F. N. Spon, London, 1996. The potential of the selective mode in contemporary design is developed further in Dean Hawkes, Koen Steemers and Jane MacDonald, *The Selective Environment*, E. & F. N. Spon, London, 2001.

SELECTIVE MODE

Offices for Apicorp
notes
1. C. Slessor, 'Sheltering Sky', *The Architectural Review*, March 1998, vol. CCIII, no. 1213, p. 34.
2. *RIBA Journal*, April 1995, 102/4.
3. F. Duffy, 'Office Interiors and Organisations – A comparative study of the relation between organisational structure and the use of interior space in sixteen office organisations', Princeton University PhD, 1974.
4. DEGW, *Planning Office Space*, Architectural Press, London, 1976.
5. K. Asfour, 'Cultural Crisis', *Architectural Review*, March 1998, vol. CCIII, no. 1213, pp. 52–60.
sources
Architectural Review, March 1998, vol. CCIII, no. 1213.
Building Design, 26 May 1995, no. 1222.

Eastgate
sources
1. Robert de Jager, et al, Special Issue: 'Sustainable Architecture', *Architecture SA*, no. 7/8, July/ August, 1997, pp. 23–29.
2. Fred Smith, 'Eastgate, Harare, Zimbabwe', *The Arup Journal*, vol. 32, no. 1, 1/1997, pp. 3–8.
3. Marian Giesen, 'Eastgate office and shopping complex, Harare, Zimbabwe', *Planning (Johannes burg)*, no. 154, November, 1997, pp. 42–45.
4. Bram Posthumus, 'Het gebouw als organism (The Building as Organism): Eastgate in Harare', *Archis*, no. 5, May, 1999, pp. 77–80.
5. Marc Gosse, et al, Special Issue: 'Villes en développement', *A plus*, no. 161, Dec/Jan, 1999/2000, pp. 64–65.

6. Liane Lefaivre, 'Making a midrise out of a termite hill', *Architecture (New York)*, vol. 89, no. 11, November, 2000, pp. 89–90.

Arup Campus

notes

1. John Harvey, quoted in *Arup Bulletin*, No 165, May 1999, p. 1.

Howlands Farm Student Housing

notes

1. Nikolaus Pevsner, *The Buildings of England: County Durham*, second edition, revised by Elizabeth Williamson, Penguin Books, Harmondsworth, 1983.

2. J. M. Richards, *The Functional Tradition*, The Architectural Press, London, 1958.

sources

Martin Spring, 'Nature studies: Howlands Farm student accommodation, Durham', *Building*, 9 June 2000.

Marzahn Low-energy Apartment Building

notes

1 John Summerson, *The Classical Language of Architecture*, revised edition, Thames and Hudson, London, 1980.

2. J. N. L. Durand, *Recueil et parallèle edifices de tous genres, anciens et modernes*, Paris, 1801.

3. W. P. Jones, 'Built form and energy needs' in A. F. C. Sherratt (ed.), *Energy Conservation and Energy Management in Buildings*, Applied Science, London, 1976.

4. Dean Hawkes, 'Building shape and energy use' in D. Hawkes and J. Owers (eds.), *The Architecture of Energy*, Longmans, Harlow, 1980. Reprinted in Dean Hawkes, *The Environmental Tradition*, E. & F. N. Spon, London, 1996.

5. Karl Fleig (ed.), *Alvar Aalto: the complete works*, 3 vols., Birkhauser Verlag, Basel, Boston, Berlin, 1971.

6. Le Corbusier, *Vers une Architecture*, Paris, 1923, English Translation *Towards a New Architecture*, by Frederick Etchells, London, 1926.

sources

Brian Cody, 'Low energy apartment building in Berlin', *The Arup Journal*, vol. 33, no. 3, 3/1998.

BedZED Sustainable Development

notes

1. Department of the Environment, Transport and the Regions, *Towards an Urban Renaissance: Final Report of the Urban Task Force*, E. & F. Spon, 1999.

2. D. Turrent, 'Hope for the Future', *RIBA Journal*, vol. 103, no. 1, January 1996, pp. 24–9.

sources

K. Long, 'Health Resort', *Building Design*, no. 1453, 25 August 2000, pp. 15–7.
K. Long, 'Green and Pleasant Land', *Building Design*, no. 1473, 9 February 2001, pp. 12–3.
A. Pearson, 'Clean Living', *Building*, vol. 265, no. 8143 (26), 30 June 2000, pp. 44–7.
Ove Arup and Partners, 'A practical solution for

sustainable living in Sutton', Concept Stage Report, July 1999.

Mont Cenis Training Centre

notes

1. R. M. Lebens (ed.), *Passive Solar Architecture in Europe: The Results of the First European Passive Solar Competition*, 1980, Architectural Press, London, pp. 92–5.

2. 'Entwicklungsgesellschaft Mont-Cenis, Fortbildungsakademie Herne', a special report on the project, published by Stadt Herne, Montan Grundstückgesellschaft, 1998.

sources

Architectural Review, vol. 206, no. 1232, October 1999, pp. 30–1 and 46–71.
Detail 'Special Issue', vol. 39, no. 3, April/May 1999, pp. 358–60.
Techniques and Architecture, no. 443, June/July 1999.
World Architecture, no. 80, October 1999, pp. 44–9.

Study Centre, Darwin College

sources

Peter Davey, 'Heart of Oak', *The Architectural Review*, October 1994, pp. 50–3.
Simon Hancock, Roger Hyde and Mick White, 'Darwin College Study Centre, Cambridge', *The Arup Journal*, vol. 33, no. 1, 1/1996, pp. 16–8.
Sabine Schnieder, 'Bibliothek in Cambridge', *Baumeister*, June 1995, pp. 33–9.

Jubilee Campus, University of Nottingham

notes

1. P. Fawcett, 'Campus Arcadia', *Architectural Review*, no. 1236, February 2000, pp. 42–7.

2. J. Palmer, 'Under Pressure', *Building Services Journal*, August 1999, pp. 24–9.

3. P. Fawcett, op. cit.

sources

J. Berry, 'Super-Efficient Mechanical Ventilation', *Indoor and Built Environment*, March–April 2000, pp. 87–96.
P. Fawcett, 'Campus Arcadia', *Architectural Review*, no. 1236, February 2000, pp. 42–7.
J. Palmer, 'Under Pressure', *Building Services Journal*, August 1999, pp. 24–9.
'Green Agenda. Hopkins & Partners at Nottingham', EcoTech 1, issue 1, *Architecture Today*, March 2000, pp. 32–36.

Cultural Centre

notes

1 S. McInstry: Tjibaou quoted in 'Sea and Sky', *Architectural Review*, no. 1222, December 1998, p. 30.

2. K. Frampton, *Studies in Tectonic Form and Culture: The Poetics of Construction in Nineteenth and Twentieth Century Architecture*, MIT Press, 1995, p. 382.

3. P. Buchanan, *Renzo Piano Building Workshop*, vol. 2, Phaidon Press, 1995, p. 192.

4. K. Frampton, op. cit., p. 382.

5. S. McInstry, op. cit. p. 36.

sources

M. Banfi and A. Guthrie, 'Kanak Cultural Centre, Nouméa, New Caledonia', *The Arup Journal*, no. 2, 1999, pp. 26–9.
M. Chown and A. Guthrie, 'The Design of a Naturally Ventilated Cultural Centre in French New Caledonia', *Proceedings of CIBSE National Conference, Brighton, 2–4 October 1994*, vol. 2, pp. 121–133.

Carmel Mountain Ranch Public Library

notes

1. Esther McCoy, Case Study Houses 1945–1962, Hennessey & Ingalls, second edition 1977.

EXCLUSIVE MODE

Helicon Building

notes

1. L. Martin and L. March, 'Land Use and Built Form', *Cambridge Research*, April 1996.

2. D. Hawkes and R. MacCormac, 'Office Form, Energy and Land Use', *RIBA Journal*, 1978.

sources

Building Services Journal, September 1996.
Building Services Journal, October 1996.
Architecture Today, no. 73, November 1996.
T. Herzog, *Solar Energy in Architecture and Urban Planning*, Prestel, Munich, 1996.

Villa VPRO Offices

notes

1. P. Davey, 'Work Ethics', *Architectural Review*, no.1232, October 1999, p. 30.

2. Peter Buchanan, *A&U*, no.9 (336), September 1998, p.48.

3. P. Stam, 'Villa VPRO', *Architectural Review*, no. 1225, March 1999, p. 42.

4. B. Lootsma, '*Pays Bas Prospective*', L'Architecture d'Aujourd'hui, September, 1996.

5. H. Ibelings, 'Supermodernism: Architecture in the Age of Globalisation', *NAI*, Amsterdam, 1998.

sources

P. Stam, 'Villa VPRO', *Architectural Review*, no. 1225, March 1999.

Beyeler Foundation Museum

notes

1. T. Markus, *Buildings and Power*, Routledge, London, 1993, p. 171.

2. R. Ryan, 'Pastoral Pavilion', *Architectural Review*, December 1997.

3. A. McDowell, A. Sedgwick, A. Smith and J. Wernick, 'Beyeler Foundation Museum, Riehen, Switzerland', *Arup Journal*, 2/1999, p. 19.

sources

P. Buchanan, *Renzo Piano Building Workshop*, vol. 2, Phaidon Press, 1995.
A. McDowell, A. Sedgwick, A. Smith and

J. Wernick, 'Beyeler Foundation Museum, Riehen, Switzerland', *Arup Journal*, 2/1999, pp. 18–21.
R. Ryan, 'Pastoral Pavilion', *Architectural Review*, December 1997, pp. 59–62.
A. Tichhauser, 'Silent Light: Piano in Basel', *Architecture Today*, no. 86, March 1998, pp. 14–20.

Byzantine Fresco Chapel Museum

notes

1. Renzo Piano, Menil Art Museum, Houston, Texas, 1986.
2. Renzo Piano, Cy Twombly Gallery, Houston, Texas, 1993.
3. Peter Rice, *An engineer imagines*, Artemis Press, London, 1993; and Andy Brown, *Peter Rice*, Thomas Telford, London, 2000.
4. Umberto Eco, *Travels in Hyperreality*, translated by William Weaver, Harcourt Brace Jovanovitch, San Diego, 1990.

sources

Catherine Slessor, 'Out of this world', *The Architectural Review*, May 1998, pp. 82–85.
Ignacio Barandiaran, Varughese Cherian, Ray Quinn, Andy Sedgwick, 'Byzantine Fresco Chapel Museum, Houston, Texas', *The Arup Journal*, vol. 33, no. 1, 1/1998.

Museum of Contemporary Art

notes

1. Josef Paul Kleihues, quoted in Andrea Mesecke and Thorsten Scheer, *Museum of Contemporary Art Chicago*, Gebr. Mann Verlag, Berlin, 1996.
2. Andrea Mesecke and Thorsten Scheer, op. cit.
3. Carl W. Conduit, *The Chicago School of Architecture*, University of Chicago Press, Chicago and London, 1964.
4. Andrea Mesecke and Thorsten Scheer, op. cit.

sources

Nicola Martin and Andrew Sedgwick, 'Chicago Museum of Contemporary Art', *The Arup Journal*, vol. 31, no. 3, 3/1996, pp. 3–5.

Walsall Art Gallery

notes

1. Robert Venturi, 'From Invention to Convention in Architecture', in I*conography and Electronics upon a Generic Architecture: A View from the Drafting Room,* MIT Press, Cambridge, Mass., 1996.
2. Brian Carter, *The Architectural Review*, May 2000, pp.62-66.
3. Mark Girouard, *Robert Smythson and the Elizabethan Country House,* Yale University Press, New Haven, 1983.

Tate Modern

notes

1. Dietmar Steiner, 'Tate Modern, London', interview with Jacques Herzog, *Domus*, 828, July/August 2000, pp. 32–43.
2. Doreen Massey, 'Bankside: International Local', in, Iwona Blazwick and Simon Wilson (eds.), *Tate Modern: the handbook,* Tate Publishing, London, 2000, pp. 24–7.

3. Dietmar Steiner, op. cit.
4. Nikolaus Pevsner, *Pioneers of Modern Design*, revised edition, Penguin Books, Harmondsworth, 1960.

sources

1. Dietmar Steiner, op. cit.
2. Tony Fretton, 'Into the void: Herzog & de Meuron's Tate Modern', *Architecture Today*, No. 109, June 2000, pp. 34–57.

Portuguese Pavilion

notes

1. Alvaro Siza, *Siza: Architectural Writings*, Antonio Angellillo (ed.), Skira, Milan, 1997.
2. Kenneth Frampton, *Alvaro Siza: Complete Works*, Electra, Milan, 1999. English edition, Phaidon Press, London, 2000.
3. *The Architectural Review*, November, 1985
4. Alvaro Siza, op. cit.

sources

Philip Jodidio, *Alvaro Siza*, Benedikt Taschen Verlag GmbH, Cologne, 1999.
Kenneth Frampton, *Alvaro Siza: Complete Works*, Electra, Milan, 1999. English edition, Phaidon Press, London, 2000.
Mike Gilroy, Fred Ilidio, Andrew Minson, Martin Walton, 'The Portuguese National Pavilion', *The Arup Journal*, vol. 34, no. 2, 2/1999.

Velodrome

sources

Mike Banfi, David Deighton, Paul Nuttall, Raj Patel, Alan Tweedie and Mohsen Zikri, 'Radsporthalle, Berlin', *Arup Journal*, vol. 32, no. 4, 4/1997, pp. 3–10.
Andy Cook, 'Buried leisure', *Building*, 16 May 1997, pp. 50–2.
Sebastian Redeke, 'Velodromo, Berlino', *Domus*, 812, February 1999, pp. 12–21.

Offices for Apicorp
Client: Apicorp
Architect: DEGW Ltd
Arup role: Structural, mechanical, electrical, public health, infrastructure, and communications engineer
Quantity surveyor: Davis Langdon & Everest

Eastgate
Project manager and building developer: Old Mutual Properties, Zimbabwe
Architect: Pearce Partnership
Arup role: Structural, mechanical, electrical, public health and civil engineer
Quantity surveyor: Hawkins Leshnick & Bath

Arup Campus
Client: Ove Arup Partnership
Architect, structural, mechanical, electrical, and public health engineer, quantity surveyor: Arup Associates
Other Arup role: Acoustic, communications, fire, and transportation engineer

Howlands Farm Student Housing
Client: Durham University Developments Ltd
Architect, structural, mechanical, electrical, and public health engineer, quantity surveyor: Arup Associates
Other Arup role: Geotechnical, acoustic, and infrastructure engineer

Marzahn Low-Energy Apartment Building
Client: Wohnungsbaugesellschaft Marzahn mbH
Architect: Assmann Salomon und Scheidt
Arup role: Structural, mechanical, electrical, public health engineer and energy consultant

BedZED Sustainable Development
Client: The Peabody Trust
Architect: Bill Dunster Architects
Arup role: Building services and building physics engineer, and energy consultant
Structural engineer: Ellis & Moore Consulting Engineers
Quantity surveyor: Gardiner & Theobald

Mont Cenis Training Centre
Client: Innenminister des Landes Nordrhein-Westfalen
Architect: Jourda & Perraudin
Associate architect: HHS Planer & Architekten
Arup role: Concept and scheme structural, mechanical, electrical, public health lighting engineer
Quantity surveyor: BDM Development

Study Centre, Darwin College
Client: Darwin College, Cambridge
Architect: Jeremy Dixon & Edward Jones
Arup role: Structural, mechanical, electrical, public health engineer
Quantity surveyor: David Langdon & Everest

Jubilee Campus, University of Nottingham
Client: University of Nottingham
Architect: Michael Hopkins and Partners
Arup role: Structural, mechanical, electrical, public health, building physics, and civil engineer
Quantity surveyor: Gardiner and Theobald
Construction manager: Bovis Midlands

Cultural Centre
Architect: Renzo Piano Structural, mechanical, electrical, public health Workshop
Arup role: Structural concept and mechanical, electrical, and public health engineer
Climate control feasibility: CSTB

Carmel Mountain Ranch Public Library
Client: Carmel Mountain Ranch Library
Architect: MW Steele Group Inc
Arup role: Structural, mechanical, electrical, and public health engineer

Helicon Building
Client: London & Manchester Assurance Co Ltd
Building user: Marks & Spencer plc
Architect: Sheppard Robson
Arup role: Structural, mechanical, electrical, public health, fire, and acoustic engineer
Quantity surveyor: Silk & Frazier

Villa VPRO Offices
Client: VPRO Broadcasting Company, Hilversum
Client representative: Heidemij Advies BV, Arnhem
Architect: MVRDV, Rotterdam
Arup role: Scheme structural, mechanical, electrical, public health engineer and site supervision
Building physics consultant: DGMR, Arnhem

Beyeler Foundation Museum
Client: Beyeler Foundation
Architect: Renzo Piano Structural, mechanical, electrical, public health Workshop
Arup role: Structural concept, scheme roof design (including glazing), mechanical, electrical, public health and lighting engineer, and energy consultant

Byzantine Fresco Chapel Museum
Client: The Menil Foundation
Architect: François de Menil
Arup role: Structural, mechanical, electrical, public health, acoustic, and communications engineer, and lighting concept

Museum of Contemporary Art
Client: Board of Trustees, Chicago Museum of Contemporary Art
Architect: Josef Paul Kleihues
Arup role: Structural, mechanical, electrical, public health, lighting, and acoustic engineer to scheme and detail design

Walsall Art Gallery
Client: Walsall Metropolitan Borough Council
Architect: Caruso St John Architects

Arup role: Structural, mechanical, electrical, public health, lighting, fire, acoustics, and communications engineer, planning supervision
Quantity surveyor: Hanscomb
Project managers: The London Group and Bucknall Austin

Tate Modern
Client: The Tate Gallery
Project manager: Stanhope Properties Ltd
Architect: Herzog & De Meuron Architekten
Associate architect: Sheppard Robson
Arup role: Structural, mechanical, electrical, public health, civil, lighting, fire, traffic/transportation, acoustic, and communications engineer, planning advice

Portuguese Pavilion
Client: Parque Expo '98
Architect: Alvaro Siza Vieira
Arup role: Scheme structural, mechanical, electrical, public health, lighting, fire, and acoustic engineer

Velodrome
Client: OSB Sportstättenbauten GmbH, Berlin
Architect: Dominique Perrault, Paris
Arup role: Structural, mechanical, electrical, public health, geotechnical, specialist lighting, communications, and acoustic engineer, quantity surveying, cost control, construction management

Many people have provided assistance in the production of this book. We are particularly grateful to Arup, who have made available the considerable resource of their archive relating to the buildings discussed in the Critical Studies. Bob Emmerson, the Chairman, has guided the project throughout and David J Brown, Editor of The Arup Journal, and Arup's Archivist, Pauline Shirley, have given day-to-day support in gaining access to material. In Cardiff we have made much use of the Architecture Library at the Welsh School of Architecture and wish to thank Sylvia Harris and her staff for their tolerance and help. As always in a project of this kind, many of the ideas and arguments derive from the conversations that we conduct daily with colleagues and students. We wish to thank them for this.

Wayne Forster
Dean Hawkes
Cardiff 2001

Picture Credits

All pictures reproduced with kind permission from Arup, except for the following:

Index